INTERACTIVE PROJECT MANAGEMENT

Pixels, People, and Process

GEEK GIRLS GUIDE

WWW.GEEKGIRLSGUIDE.COM

New Riders

VOICES THAT MATTER™

For our families: Laura and Merrick, and Jeremy, Trixie, and Theo, who patiently supported us as we worked long hours to finish the book. We couldn't have done it without you.

And to the past and current Clockworkers, the smart, talented, and invaluable guinea pigs that improved and fine-tuned our process.

Interactive Project Management: Pixels, People, and Process
Nancy Lyons and Meghan Wilker

New Riders

Find us on the Web at: www.newriders.com
To report errors, please send a note to errata@peachpit.com

New Riders is an imprint of Peachpit, a division of Pearson Education.

Project Editor: Michael J. Nolan
Development Editors: Margaret S. Anderson/Stellarvisions
Project Manager: Lyz Nagan
Production Editor: Cory Borman
Copyeditor: Gretchen Dykstra
Proofreader: Jan Seymour
Cover Designer: Aren Straiger
Interior Designer: Charlene Charles-Will
Compositor: Danielle Foster
Indexer: Joy Dean Lee

ISBN 13: 978-0-321-81515-6
ISBN 10: 0-321-81515-7

2 16

Printed and bound in the United States of America

Acknowledgements

This book is the result of a huge effort by many people over a great amount of time. We've been lucky enough to work with amazing colleagues, partners, and clients over the years. Every project clarified our thinking—and our determination.

First and foremost, we have to thank **Chuck Hermes**, **Kurt Koppelman**, and **Michael Koppelman**. With Nancy, they founded Clockwork Active Media, where we shaped the vision and did the work that refined our thinking and process. That this book exists is a testament to their insight, trust, and dedication.

We'd also like to give a shout-out to the Clockworkers who directly contributed to the book: **Selah Ben-Haim**, **Ben Beuchler**, **Telari Bohrnsen**, **Mollie Clancy**, **Lloyd Dalton**, **Justin 'Dez' Dessonville**, **Dave Dohmeier**, **Ryan Evans**, **Matt Gray**, **Eric Hanson**, **Kjrsten Holt**, **Julie Horton**, **Matt 'Hank' Kiedrowski**, **Andrew Leaf**, **Ryan Loomis**, **Rett Martin**, **Kevin O'Brien**, **Eryn O'Neil**, **Michael Opperman**, **Ruth Rosengren**, **Whitney Shaw**, and **Luke Vestrum**. Special thanks and a high-five to **Micah Spieler**, who designed our gorgeous book graphics.

Reaching back into history, thank you to the clients, partners, and colleagues of Bitstream Underground, where we first started working together, and where the seed for this book was planted.

Thank you to **Amanda Costello** and the board of MinneWebCon who invited us to speak at the 2011 conference, and to **Kris Layon** for advice and guidance on writing a book and who, without our knowledge, went out of his way to invite his book editor to see us speak there. Thanks to said book editor, **Michael Nolan**, for showing up, liking what he saw, and inviting us on this book-writing adventure. Thank you to the extended team at Peachpit: **Margaret Anderson**, **Glenn Bisignani**, **Cory Borman**, **Gretchen Dykstra**, **Danielle Foster**, **Joy Dean Lee**, **Jan Seymour**, and **Charlene Will**. You shepherded the book through to completion and thoughtfully made it a reality.

Thank you to **Julie Allinson** and **eyebobs**, who named a pair of eyeglasses after us (!!!) and let us use them on the book cover.

To our early readers—**Jamie Jacobsen**, **Margaret McInerny**, and **Mahtab Rezai**— whose critical feedback was helpful and whose pats on the back were appreciated. And thank you to **Tiger Beaudoin**, who let us use his picture as our representative client; lookin' good! And much appreciation goes out to **Jesse James Garrett**, who allowed us to adapt his seminal illustration for the book.

Thanks to the vibrant Minneapolis interactive community. We're grateful to be a part of it.

It's impossible to write a book about project management without being managed, and really, the only person that could manage us is **Lyz Nagan**. Thanks to her for the gentle (and sometimes not-so-gentle) nudges, late night emails, and all-day meetings. Not to mention spending two days locked in a cabin with us.

Nancy: Do you mind if I say a personal thank you?

Meghan: Only if I can do the same.

Nancy: Of course, but you can't thank the Vampire Diaries.

Meghan: Why not? It helped me recover from some pretty tough chapters.

Nancy: Our work often takes us away from the people we love the most, and writing this book was no exception. With as much affection and gratitude as can be conveyed in words on a page, I want to thank my partner, **Laura**, and my son, **Merrick**.

Meghan: Yes. And thanks to my husband, **Jeremy**, for his support and encouragement. I'm grateful to have him as a husband and co-parent. Thanks also to my children, **Trixie** and **Theo**, for putting up with mama being away so much and for snuggling me tight whenever I'm home.

Nancy: Also, I know this might go without saying—but it shouldn't—I want to thank you, Meghan.

Meghan: Oh man, is this the emotional part?

Nancy: Yes, and you can't stop me. Work can be really intense and stressful, and we often get so busy that we use up our emotional and physical energy. But the thing that makes people—myself included—happiest at work is having a friend there. And, Meghan, you're the person that makes it easy and more enjoyable for me to do my work.

Meghan: Right back at ya, sister.

Preface

In our many years in the interactive industry, we've witnessed more than a few projects become train wrecks. It's happened in large and small advertising agencies, software companies, and digital agencies alike. Most of these wrecks could have been avoided.

In nearly every case, the problem was that nothing held the team together, which led to clashes between stakeholders. We've seen the client-side project manager who was relatively isolated try to manage the marketing and IT departments. Sometimes the IT department resented the marketing team over initiatives that IT felt they should either own or heavily influence. And other times the marketing team came to resent the IT department because IT controlled the product's delivery, and in doing so created a bottleneck.

We've seen creative professionals steamroll technologists, technologists ignore strategy, and strategists curb creativity.

We've seen companies hire freelancers specifically for their interactive expertise, without giving them the authority to guide the internal teams who needed help in the first place. And over the years we've met many leaders who didn't understand digital products or their medium-specific requirements, which left teams working in a vacuum.

And in these scenarios, no one was willing to say, "I don't know what's happening or what *should* be happening." Yet it's true. And under *any* of these conditions—let alone under *several* of these conditions—it's difficult to get anything done well.

What was the missing link? A well-understood process and effective project management.

A good process unites clients, leaders, teams, and project managers. It gives everyone a shared understanding, which is exactly what's needed to stay on track. Really, this book should be called "A Client, Leader, Team, and Project Manager's Guide to Avoiding Train Wrecks." But for some reason our publisher rejected that title.

Process, and project management, save the day

Projects fail because stakeholder expectations aren't met or promises are broken. But this is solvable. A good process makes people work better—and together. Effective project management means that the expectations and promises are established and realized.

A clear company-wide process means creative, strategic, and technological thinking can come together successfully. And a standard industry-wide process means that all stakeholders know what to expect and what to ask for.

What you'll learn

This is a guide to understanding and launching successful interactive projects. It's more of a how-to-think guide than a how-to-do guide. While we've included useful tips and advice throughout the book, the primary lessons are about how to approach people, tasks, stages, and phases within a project.

The first half of the book outlines the role of the interactive project manager and our approaches to project management. Both the role and approach focus on the people side of things. We discuss what it takes to be an effective project manager and how to navigate the often unpaved road from project initiation to launch. In these chapters, you'll see the words collaboration and communication a lot.

The second half of the book walks you through the project management methodology we use at Clockwork Active Media, the digital agency where we work. It illustrates how to apply the role and approaches discussed in the first half to an actual project. It establishes phases and deliverables that organize the thinking into actions.

No matter what environment you're in—a digital agency, an advertising agency, or an in-house marketing team—you can integrate our methodology. The tools and software you use are almost irrelevant; the important thing is how you *think* about and approach projects and people.

How we got here

Our process evolved from many aspects of our work. We looked at our successes (and failures) on past projects, observed how work was done in a variety of environments, and interviewed people in our own company—and at others. We pulled from existing models of project management and drew on prevailing ideas about work, culture, and people.

We asked questions like: What do clients, technologists, and creative teams need? What parts of projects tend to be challenging to clients and the internal team? How can we facilitate the best possible work as efficiently as possible (for both clients and ourselves)? Where is there value in existing methods, and where are there gaps?

Actually, we *keep* asking these questions to ensure that the process is still serving us well. The ultimate goal is to create work that's a perfect balance of quality and efficiency.

A common starting point

Before we continue, let's make sure we're all on the same page. (Wow. It's kind of fun to say that in a book. We actually *are* on the same page.)

We believe that a good process

- Serves people, doesn't thwart them
- Enables creativity, doesn't kill it
- Evolves constantly
- Is no substitute for thinking

Okay. If you're on board, read on.

Contents

CHAPTER 1 The Interactive Industry   **1**
It's people. It's technology. It's everywhere.

CHAPTER 2 Interactive Project Management 101   **15**
A new job for a unique industry

CHAPTER 3 Emotional Intelligence   **27**
Technology doesn't drive projects, people do

CHAPTER 4 Communication   **41**
Right message. Right medium. Right time.

Introduction

Interactive projects require a different approach and an industry-specific process. The challenge is complex: Interactive projects are chaotic by nature, yet some sense of order must be imposed. The key is a good process, and the key that is a focus on people.

From every angle, interactive projects are about people—the people who commission, design, develop, deploy, and use the end products.

The people side of projects requires full-team collaboration and effective communication. The project itself requires thoughtful planning and *many* lists outlining each and every feature. All this, which may seem labor intensive, actually saves time and energy, and improves quality, success rates, and team members' and clients' satisfaction.

Below are the mantras for tackling interactive projects. They give you a framework for thinking about and approaching the work, so your subsequent actions will be effective.

INTERACTIVE PROJECT MANAGEMENT

- Project managers think, analyze, communicate, and motivate.
- Interactive project management is a leadership role.
- A good project manager plans proactively, reacts appropriately, communicates actively, and observes vigilantly.
- Interactive project managers should be personable, detail oriented, naturally communicative, and active online.

PIXELS

- The interactive industry creates living products that are *used,* not consumed.
- Plan for change; technology is always evolving.
- Interactive products unite creative technology and technological creativity.
- The success of a product is measured by users' experiences with it.

PEOPLE

- Recognize and work with people's emotions, not against them.
- Care about your team, your clients, and your work.
- Be collaborative, open, clear, and thorough.
- Effective communication is essential: Think about what precisely needs to be communicated and the best way to deliver *that* message.

PROCESS

- Processes enable work, they don't obstruct it.
- The process isn't just for project managers—it's for everybody.
- Planning means greater freedom to find the *right* solution.
- Define what you're doing and why: Establish parameters and requirements; state goals and strategies.

About the authors

Nancy Lyons

Think strategically, act thoughtfully, be a good human.

Nancy works at the intersection of technology, community, and people. As a leader and technologist, she creates solutions that further community and business goals by meeting the needs of individuals. Her guiding philosophy is that a human-centered approach to technology is the only way to get results that make a difference. Problem solving is about empowerment: motivated people create good products. Nancy supports clients and teams by fostering a collaborative, idea-driven culture that nurtures creativity and brainpower.

Nancy is President/CEO of Clockwork Active Media, a leading digital agency specializing in designing and developing business solutions for web, mobile, and other digital environments. She speaks extensively about work culture, social media, technology, and leadership and has been locally and nationally recognized for her role as owner and CEO of Clockwork. Nancy serves on the National Board of Directors at The Family Equality Council.

Meghan Wilker

Meghan specializes in using strategy, technology, and process to bring people and products together. Her public speaking, writing, and outreach guides individuals and businesses to develop smart digital products. Whether she's managing a team or mentoring students, she believes that technology creates endless opportunities to make life easier and to produce meaningful connections. She empowers users to pro-actively engage with the web by being aware, educated, and attentive and spearheads dialogue that drives evolution within the interactive community.

Meghan is the VP, Managing Director at Clockwork Active Media, a digital agency specializing in designing and developing business solutions for web, mobile, and other digital environments. She's a contributing writer at GTDtimes.com, and was named as a "Woman to Watch" by the Minneapolis/St. Paul Business Journal.

1

THE INTERACTIVE INDUSTRY

It's people. It's technology. It's everywhere.

Despite a relatively short history, the products created by the inter-active industry are now ubiquitous in our daily lives, from how we obtain news to how we communicate with our loved ones to how we work with our colleagues. Understanding this landscape is critical to creating products that are effective for both clients and end users.

In this chapter, we'll discuss

- The interactive industry and its products
- Its evolution from software development and advertising
- Manifestos: guides for clients, leaders, and teams

The interactive industry is a little like advertising and a little like software, but it's also something altogether different. As organizations, interactive agencies are often viewed as peers of advertising or marketing, while their deliverables are often viewed like software. But neither of those perspectives are entirely accurate—especially when it comes to process. Before jumping into managing interactive projects, let's look at what the industry is, how it evolved, and what stakeholders should know about it.

The interactive industry

So what characterizes the interactive world as an industry? Ultimately, it's the unique relationship between the end product and the end user.

What does *interactive* mean?

Technically speaking, interactive means just that: something you can interact with, and have an affect on. You act and the system responds, by design.

The interactive industry produces digital products that advance client business goals through effective interactions.

What the products do, how they're used, who uses them, and what they look like varies widely from project to project. In fact, those are all the details that teams determine when working on a project. It's why we wrote a book.

Pixels

HELLO, INTERNET

The first popular web browser, Mosaic, was introduced in 1993.

In the last 15 years, both the interactive industry and its products have evolved dramatically.

While websites were certainly around in the early 1990s, they didn't become mainstream until the mid-'90s. In those days, interactive encompassed websites, but more often it meant things like CD-ROMs (remember those?). Mainly because, aside from animated GIFs and links, browsers and Internet connections couldn't handle much of what we consider interactions today.

As the technology evolved and e-commerce emerged, the industry was crazed about what *could* be built online—few were thinking clearly about what they *should* build online. We built things that the audience wasn't ready for, and we overvalued them to an extreme. As an example, while it was possible to buy and sell things online in the '90s, most people weren't yet comfortable with the technology. So the number of e-commerce sites far exceeded the number of people willing to use them.

During the bust of the early 2000s, companies folded and merged and everyone realized that "If you build it, they will come" wasn't a business plan. (One could argue that recently we've been enduring a new, equally ridiculous "social boom" but that's another book.)

As the technology and we, as users, have matured and high-bandwidth connections have become nearly ubiquitous, the concept of interactive has expanded to include complex interactions on websites, mobile sites and applications, kiosks, digital installations, and more. Today, the notion of CD-ROMs is antiquated. Who knows what interactive will encompass in 10 years?

The rush to do *anything* as long as it's online should be over. Now, we need to reflect on what we learned from the boom and bust of the last decade, and focus on defining how we, as in industry, can deliver work that brings value to clients and end users alike.

People

Interactive isn't just about programmers. And it's not just about user experience architects, interaction designers, or content strategists, either. These roles are important, but what's most important is that they work in concert toward a shared goal. For too long, that point has been lost among the chest beating of individual disciplines. That needs to change. Many people from a number of expertise areas move a project to completion, and the interactive project manager helps keep them all aligned.

Who are these people and what are their roles in the process? Let us explain.

Figure 1.1 on the following spread illustrates many possible roles on a project, each as a separate person. Every one isn't required for every project, and, in some cases, you may have one person fulfilling more than one role (for example, the designer may also be the front-end developer).

Project Roles

Account Strategist
She articulates the goals and strategies that govern and direct every expertise areas' contribution to the project. She directs the Research & Planning phase, and as the project unfolds, keeps people and activities focused on scope and goals. Sometimes called business analyst.

Back-end Developer
She writes the code that powers the end product. She is responsible for designing and constructing software to meet project requirements, and translates the written features into a working artifact. Sometimes called software engineer or programmer.

Client
The person or team for whom the work is being done. Frequently, it's an external client. If you're with an in-house team, it could be another department within the company or one person with whom you work.

Content Strategist
She provides strategic guidance to ensure that content is clear, concise, and focused on business and user goals. She informs the user experience architecture, design, and site development. And she creates a long-term plan for content maintenance and development.

Creative Lead
He's responsible for setting the creative vision. He's the guiding eye for the project's creative elements and works closely with the designer to execute the creative vision. Sometimes called creative director or art director.

Designer
He brings together the information architecture and creative vision into mockups that are presented to the client. He meets often with front-end developers to discuss intended interactions and functionality. Sometimes called interaction designer.

Front-end Developer
She is responsible for creating interfaces. She uses a variety of markup and scripting languages to apply the design concepts and information architecture to individual screens, producing a consistent and easy-to-use end product.

FIGURE 1.1
The numerous roles that make up a project team.

Production Lead

He oversees front-end production to ensure design and functionality come together in seamless interfaces that utilize appropriate technology. He fosters big-picture ideation, problem solving, and communication to achieve effective and successful user experiences.

Project Manager

This all-knowing leader manages every aspect of the project definition and delivery: tasks, roles, and deliverables. He ensures that every factor of the project is aligned with the plan and goals and shepherds work, leads people, and brings everything together to meet precisely in the end product.

Relationship Manager

This person or team is someone that the client talks to about the project, but who isn't directly involved in day-to-day work. He focuses on keeping the client feel heard and engaged. Sometimes called account team, account director, or account manager.

System Administrator

He manages the server-side hardware and software that make the end product available to its users (like servers and hosting). He plays a critical role leading up to and after launch day. He could be internal, client-side, or third-party.

Tech Lead

He oversees the technological vision, thinking, and planning on a project. He is fluent in both business and technical communication, able to translate client needs into requirements and explain technical concepts to others.

Tester

He is responsible for verifying that features and functionality align with the requirements, plans, and goals established throughout the project. He confirms the design, user experience architecture, and features work according to plan.

User Experience Architect

He documents the audience's needs and outlines the structure and organization of the end product. He bridges design and functionality to ensure that strategic and technical considerations result in effective user experiences. Sometimes called information architect.

THINK ABOUT: Interactions vs. calls to action

Just because something is displayed on the web, or on a screen, doesn't mean it's interactive. Banner ads and emails are more advertising than interactive. While they're constructed of pixels, the call to action is generally a specific request. Y'know, the good old, "Click here." The processes in most agencies can handle the creation of those things just fine. What we're talking about here are digital products that users can interact with in more complex ways: websites, applications, digital installations, and kiosks.

Process

Because the industry and its products have evolved so quickly, no single process has become the standard. When advertising agencies began integrating digital into their existing processes for delivering traditional media work (television, radio, and print) one type of process formed. As technology firms wrote code and extended software products online, a different process emerged.

But neither of those approaches is a perfect fit for the unique nature of the interactive industry. In the coming chapters, we'll outline a methodology that we've refined over the past 15 years—one that's been shaped by our experience developing software and web applications, leading digital agencies, collaborating with and working for advertising agencies, and working with diverse teams of creative professionals and technologists.

Hi there. I'm Nancy, President and CEO of Clockwork Active Media. Throughout the book I'll share ideas about leadership and work culture as they relate to interactive projects.

And, I'm Meghan. VP, Managing Director at Clockwork Active Media. I'll be sharing insights about managing and executing the approaches we talk about.

Evolution from software and advertising

As the interactive discipline emerged, it landed between two industries: software and advertising. This was in part because it borrowed a little from each. Software developers knew the technology; advertising agencies understood creative work.

In the early 1990s, the development of interactive products was happening mostly within the software industry. This made sense: The product relied on technology and information that few people outside of software engineering understood.

In the late 1990s and early 2000s, advertising agencies began to get into digital media. This also made sense: Interactive deliverables were (and are) often used for traditional marketing purposes like brand awareness, commerce, and promotions. "Integration" became the name of the game, and to be integrated agencies either built interactive departments from within, or partnered with (or bought) the digital agencies that were emerging around that time as well.

But while the association with both software and advertising made sense in the early days, it doesn't make much sense today. The road from the '90s to today has been difficult for clients, agencies, and end users: broken promises, busted budgets, cultural clashes between interactive and traditional media teams, and that whole Flash microsite thing that went on for far too long.

The lines are blurry—as software is delivered online, and as the complexity of websites increases, it's hard to say what is advertising and what is software, what's message and what's product.

Inside that blurry area is where interactive exists. Interactive products are both technological and creative; they're both software and advertising; they're both functional and fun.

The creation of interactive media is different from both software and advertising. It's time to recognize that difference, and establish a new way of delivering work, separate from those two industries. The industry is mature enough that we can say—with confidence—what works and what doesn't.

FACT: Animation is the opposite of interaction

Often, when people think "interactive" they think of something that moves. But animation is the opposite of interactive; a user's engagement with animation is passive. It's something to watch. That's okay if it's the desired effect. But if the goal is to get a user to interact, animation may not be the best way to achieve it.

ALWAYS REMEMBER

Unless an interactive product is created thoughtfully, with purpose, and effectively meets the needs of the user, it's not a solution, it's just a pretty thing on the Internet. It's important for all clients, agencies, and users to understand this.

Where we are now

It's an exciting time to work on interactive projects. The technology has evolved. The audience has grown. The explosion of social media has engaged a larger number of people online than ever before. Clients understand the value of interactive products now more than ever and are increasingly eager to invest in interactive solutions.

Now it's time, as an industry, to define what good interactive work is and how projects should be produced.

We're all in this together, so whether you're commissioning, building, or using a website or app, it's critical to know what characterizes the discipline. As the Goonies would say, "This is our time."

Over the years and through hundreds of projects, we've come to some key realizations that inform how we define, develop, and deploy interactive projects. These are just a few of the points that make interactive a little different than the industries from which it evolved.

The truths

INTERACTIVE PRODUCTS ARE USED, NOT CONSUMED. Users don't passively consume digital products the way they listen to a radio advertisement. They read, click, and *do* things. And sometimes the thing they do isn't at all what you wanted or expected them to do.

SCOPE MUST BE CLEARLY AND REALISTICALLY DEFINED. Scope is the hardest thing to control on an interactive project, even more so than in traditional media. Documents must outline exactly what's being produced, why it's being produced, and how its success will be measured—anything short of this and the project will suffer.

SCOPE CAN'T BE DEFINED IN A PROPOSAL. And that's all there is to it.

- *Clients:* Stop demanding that the most critical thinking should happen before the team has even had a chance to dig into the specifics of your project.

- *Agencies:* Stop acting like it's possible to deliver absolute numbers before you've had a chance to do your homework.

- *Everyone:* Stop expecting the pitch to take the place of process. The biggest **wow** should come from a successful deliverable. Not from the big show you do at a pitch meeting.

EVERYONE OWNS THE PROJECT. There's no mastermind who deserves all the praise. Interactive projects require evenly distributed respect among team members. This isn't just so everyone feels good (although that's important, too); it's because each area of expertise is legitimately necessary and just as important as the other.

THINK ABOUT: Beyond the pitch

Traditionally, agencies make a big push at pitch time. Late nights and long weekends are spent on behalf of the primary goal: to land a client. Rather, the big push should be to launch the product. The celebration should come with the completion of the project, not the completion of the pitch. The solution is what's really worth high-fiving about.

The challenges

FREE IS A TEMPTING PRICE. The proliferation of free and low-cost tools is both a blessing and a curse. While there are many ways to build products (mostly websites) for free, it takes time, thought, and expertise to create end products that are good and effective. These tools can create the perception that interactive is easy, and should be cheap. But some solutions are more complicated than a free service can provide, and free is never really free.

IT'S NEVER DONE. Interactive projects don't end when the project is delivered. Products live on long after launch day and require maintenance or updates. Technology changes, content must be updated, users give feedback, and clients' needs change. Unlike an advertisement, you don't get to crank out a fresh one each time. Often, a product will need to live—and evolve—for several years beyond launch.

IT'S FULL OF FADS. As with other very important things (like fashion and reality television) the interactive industry is full of fads. People get really excited by new innovations that seem cool. They fall in love with trends. This presents a challenge when the latest thing really isn't the best way to achieve the client's goals.

THERE'S A KNOWLEDGE GAP. There are a lot of client-side stakeholders on nearly every project. They're experts in their business but don't always understand the interactive industry or what's being built. Clients need products to solve business problems, but part of the problem is that they don't always know what's possible or effective. This gap in knowledge presents a challenge, but not an insurmountable one (read on).

THINK ABOUT: Internet vs. web

Often, people use the words *web* and *Internet* interchangeably. But this is an inaccurate characterization. The Internet is a giant network of interconnected networks. So basically it's a bunch of computers that talk to each other. The web is how we access information stored on these networks or computers—generally via a browser—but now we're seeing more and more of it via mobile interface. This distinction, and precise language in general, is important in interactive work.

Manifestos

The three primary participants in the process of creating interactive work are leadership, clients, and team members.

LEADERSHIP represents the executives and decision makers within advertising or digital agencies. They're not the specialists, but they're making decisions that directly affect the team that produces interactive products.

CLIENTS are the people who commission the work. Clients can be from an outside company that hires an agency or from another department. In either case, they're the people who need the work done.

TEAM MEMBERS are the interactive specialists: designers, developers, writers, and other pixel-pushers. They may work inside an agency or be a department inside a company.

The collective goal of these three groups is shared—to create a successful end product—but what they need, have a right to, and look for going into a project differs.

Dear leadership

KNOW AND VALUE INTERACTIVE. Interactive work is very different from traditional media production. It requires a different skill set, a different approach, and different ways to measure success. Once you embrace this and adapt to the specific requirements of interactive projects, your products will be much better.

HIRE WELL. Because interactive is *by rule* collaborative, you need to hire people who subscribe wholly to that premise. One expert can't value his expertise over any other. Don't let someone who has granular and intimate knowledge of technology be condescending to other team members. On the flip side, don't let a creative director shove the noncreative types around. Avoiding those behaviors starts with who you hire and what you tolerate as a culture.

A LONE DEVELOPER ISN'T AN INTERACTIVE DEPARTMENT. Interactive projects necessitate a group of people who all come to the project from different perspectives. Throwing a design over the wall for production doesn't work. Contributions from a designer, a user experience architect, a front-end developer, and testers are all required to make a completely thought-through product.

DON'T DICTATE, COLLABORATE

Yes, developers know technology. But they also know how to use technology creatively, and they're rarely given the credit they deserve for being creative thinkers. Don't wait until the end to involve them; your project is better when programmers and creative professionals collaborate.

USERS DON'T WANT AN EXPERIENCE. THEY WANT TO DO SOMETHING. Any content or design that gets in the user's way is a waste of the client's money. To meet users' needs and bring them closer to the information or products they're looking for, you have to spend time understanding them.

Dear clients

ASK HOW AGENCIES GET WORK DONE. When you're considering which agency to hire for your next project, ask how they get work done. They should have an answer, and they should be able to explain it in a way that you understand. If they don't, move on. Quickly.

KNOW WHAT YOU'RE GETTING. No matter your level of technical knowledge, you have every right to understand the deliverables you're getting from an agency. *Understand* is the operative word. If you don't understand, ask questions. Get answers.

MEASURE RESULTS. In the past, brand awareness was a reasonable goal for an ad campaign, but now, the ways in which products are used and their effectiveness can be more precisely measured. Require this of your team.

BE PREPARED TO PARTICIPATE. The team developing your work—whether in-house or an external agency—needs your knowledge and expertise. Don't expect—or tolerate—an interactive team that disappears for a few months and comes back with something you need. Expect to give lots of input along the way.

Dear team members

BE INVOLVED. Be actively engaged throughout every stage of a project. You have the right to know why certain decisions are made and how the project evolves. This puts you in the best position to act appropriately and in the best interest of the client and the end product.

LEARN HOW TO TALK ABOUT WHAT YOU DO. Every role within a project is a specialty, which means that others may not know exactly what you do or how you do it. Figure out how to communicate what you do and what you need to clients and other team members clearly, effectively, and without condescension.

TIP: **Encourage clients**

At times, clients may *assume* they won't understand the technology or the intricate details of a project. They may be intimidated by the process or by their lack of knowledge (whether real or perceived). This isn't good for you, them, or the project. Help get them to a point where they feel comfortable with all the information. They're sabotaging themselves from the get-go by thinking that it's over their head. It's your job to change their minds.

TREAT THE CLIENT'S MONEY LIKE YOUR OWN. When you're working on a project, the client is on your team. Put yourself in the client's shoes and act as if the client's values, vision, and money are your own. Make products that exceed your personal standards and build the product as if it's yours. Make decisions and spend time as if you're paying for it.

DON'T SETTLE FOR AN INEFFECTIVE PROCESS. If the process by which your team completes work needs improvement, do what you can to make a change. Ineffective processes compromise clients' happiness and bottom lines; that's something everyone understands—and wants to prevent. Bring it up with your team and talk about how to make improvements. Never settle.

What's coming up

In the chapters that follow, we'll explore interactive project management as a job and a discipline, and we'll outline a process that will adapt to *any* interactive project. Whether you're a client, a current (or aspiring) interactive project manager, a member of an interactive team, or an agency executive, you'll see the thinking that guides and shapes the delivery of a successful interactive product.

Bringing all the components together—clients, goals, users, features, technology, and creativity—requires precision, rigor, and flexibility.

Once you figure out how to unite these disparate elements (hint: keep reading), interactive projects—and the resulting products—will be more effective.

2

INTERACTIVE PROJECT MANAGEMENT 101

A new job for a unique industry

We're all familiar with the term *project management* and can probably give a rough definition of the discipline. But what it looks like in action—and what it should be in the interactive industry—is not well understood. Yet.

In this chapter, we'll discuss

- How we define interactive project management
- Required skills for managing real-world interactive projects
- Critical tasks that drive action
- The qualities of a good project manager

On interactive projects the project manager is the epicenter of activity. She is the all-knowing, all-seeing eye. She anticipates the needs of the team members and solves their problems before they can blink. She is a stealthy ninja, ready to strike with precision at a moment's notice, rapidly refocusing as she fights off the attacking gang of risks and roadblocks.

Defining interactive project management

If you seek out project management resources, you're likely to come across lengthy tomes like the *Project Management Body of Knowledge* (PMBOK), PMP certification, and holy wars over software development methods like waterfall versus agile (and can we please agree that *scrum* is just a terrible word?). It's not that those things are wrong. It's just that in some ways they're too much, and in others they're not enough.

Interactive, as a discipline, has emerged and evolved so quickly that industry-specific standards around how to manage projects haven't yet been established.

What is it?

**MANAGING
ISN'T**

Done poorly, project management looks a lot like email shuffling and calendar making.

The discipline of interactive project management aligns a complex assortment of factors to create effective end products that must evolve to *remain* effective. It requires special attention to

- Numerous expertise areas working on the same thing at the same time

- Clients who have varying degrees of knowledge about, and interest in, technology

- Technology that changes daily

- Business objectives and project goals that must be accounted for at every step

- End users who are an amorphous group of stakeholders with a variety of needs

Picture an orchestra (Figure 2.1)—a group of people performing independent tasks, in concert, under the direction of a conductor. It's just like that on an interactive project. The project manager is the conductor; the diverse team members are the musicians; technology and tools are the instruments; the audience members are the end users; the project goals are the symphony itself.

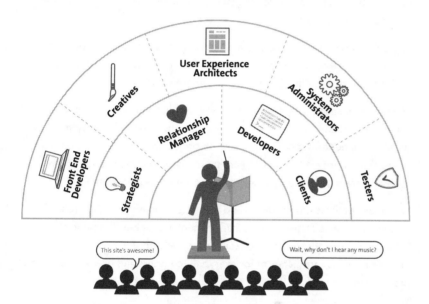

FIGURE 2.1
The project manager is the center of a project. She directs disparate people and activities and brings them together to produce a successful, synchronized end product.

On the surface, this all sounds relatively straightforward, but there's intricacy in the underlying components and how they interact. Effective interactive project management requires juggling these complex factors.

THINK ABOUT: Job titles vs. project roles

The role that people have on a project may differ from the title on their business card. This book focuses on project roles. Team members might have multiple roles on a project (perhaps the creative lead is also the designer, or one person is doing both front-end and back-end development). The only hard-and-fast rule is this: the project manager must not take on any other project role. Why? Because to manage the project properly requires maintaining an overall view of the project at all times. The project manager must always be managing.

Where is it?

Interactive project management happens in a variety of places and is executed by an equally diverse group of people. The typical scenario that we reference throughout this book is a full-scale interactive agency with a complete team of interactive professionals including the project manager, strategists, coders, designers, front-end developers, and testers.

This isn't always the case. Creative agencies might have an interactive group (or individual). And technology or noncreative firms may have an interactive department (or individual) working on in-house projects.

The project manager might work exclusively within an interactive group or might have broader responsibilities. Someone who has a different primary role, such as designer or director, might take on project management responsibilities to drive a project through. Where there is a separation between client and agency, there is often a project manager responsible for each "side."

Within any of these environments and no matter who is playing the role of project manager, effective project management is possible. The principles in this book are not only for a full team or people with "Project Manager" on their business cards. They're for everyone to understand how to get projects done.

The role of interactive project manager is vital to any company that delivers digital work; it's not a low- or mid-level position. This needs to be established from the top down. It has to be built into the company culture. Acknowledging the project manager's voice, recognizing her role as one of leadership, and valuing her as much as creative professionals and developers are valued must be institutionalized and practiced by everyone from the top of the organization down.

It's a set of critical skills

Interactive project management is a constant mix of hard and soft skills, macro and micro assessing, thinking and acting, being proactive and reactive.

THINKING. Many people see the other project contributors—developers, designers, writers—as the brains and the project manager as a conduit of information. Not the case. Seeing an interactive project through requires constant and critical thinking. The project manager receives, processes, aggregates, and makes sense of tons of pieces of information at every step. Thinking is the heartbeat of the job.

ANALYZING. Constant analysis of a project is mandatory. Even with a rock solid team and a stellar process in place, a project requires thoughtful attention. Assessing all the parts, getting to the bottom of problems, and seeing through what *appears* to be happening to what is *actually* happening are just a few of the ways analysis comes into play.

COMMUNICATING. A project manager spends most, if not all, of her day communicating: emails, phone calls, conversations, instant messages. Plus, there's a lot of nonverbal communication: facial expressions, moods, body language. A project manager has to be aware of what's being communicated—explicitly and implicitly—all the time. She has to make sense of all the information and deliver it in universal and productive ways. That means constantly listening, translating, and re-communicating information to team members and clients.

MOTIVATING. Project managers spend a good part of every day ensuring that things are moving along. And not just moving, but moving *in the right direction*: aligning people toward a common goal, adjusting when things are veering off course, and making sure people are going at the right pace. This all requires motivation. This will mean different things to different people, but having an arsenal of motivational techniques is important. And using them wisely and appropriately is a must.

> A good project manager can do the job with nothing more than a pencil and a piece of paper. Her real tools are her thinking, analyzing, communicating, and motivating.

It's also a set of critical tasks

All the skills listed are important, but they're no good without action.

Planning proactively: Forecasting the route, resources, and realities

MANAGING ISN'T

Project management isn't limited to making calendars and assigning tasks. If you don't think appropriately about tasks, you end up with a meaningless collection of dates, resources, and tasks. The real work lies in managing all the stuff that inevitably happens to jeopardize the details you've outlined and planned.

This is one of the most critical project management responsibilities. Forecasting provides a general idea of what's going to happen and when, so the team doesn't lose time trying to figure out what happens next.

The project manager needs to see where things are going before getting there, and stay about three steps ahead of everyone else. Along all points of a project, the project manager is looking at the 3-day, 10-day and end-date outlook. And keeping a full 360-degree view on things.

Managing a project starts with outlining how it will actually happen. At Clockwork, we view our process like a skeleton: a framework on which the body of each project rests. The bones don't dictate precisely what the body will look like—but they do ensure that it is built upon a solid core. What the project manager has to figure out is the exact body of each project, asking themselves: How can we best bring this project to life? What are the specific details that will get the project moving in the right direction and lead it to the desirable outcome?

Asking questions—and making a plan—isn't something the project manager does once. It's something to be done every day, *because nothing ever goes according to the original plan.*

Reacting appropriately: Problem solving and adjusting

Proactive planning provides a general idea of what might happen and what may derail the project, but, inevitably, other things will impact the project along the way.

It's critical to know how to react appropriately and make necessary adjustments when unexpected things happen. And unexpected things always will happen—it's the nature of the beast. No one else on the team has her head around the entire project like the project manager.

The two most common elements that the project manager will react to are problems (something went wrong!) and new developments (something changed!).

Problems

Sometimes they're easy to spot, but sometimes problems are subtle and tricky to see. To anticipate problems, think about

- Who might be able to identify problems, both in-house and client-side

- What questions to ask to isolate potential problems

When a problem arises, think about

- Whether this problem is part of a larger pattern or a one-off issue. If it's a recurring problem, what is the source?

- What part of the problem, if any, needs to be communicated to the client

- What needs to be done to keep work moving forward

New developments

Developments occur as a project unfolds. These could involve new technology, new resources, or new requirements. While these are positive, they can still have a negative impact on the scope or timing of the project and need to be managed accordingly. Think about

- What parts of the project a singular development affects

- Whether it requires additional face-to-face discussions

- Whether it should be communicated to the client and, if so, when and how

There are some things that project managers, no matter how awesome they are, can't be expected to see before they happen. This doesn't mean they're bad or that the team failed. It is impossible to identify

- Whether new technology that is better suited to the project *will be* developed

- Every software option

- What a client will change her mind about (this will definitely happen)

Communicating actively: Connecting the dots to avoid pitfalls

With any interactive project, many things are happening simultaneously. That's how it should be. But sometimes two groups, or two people, or two problems should be connected. An effective project manager will spot gaps in communication or expectations, and she'll know when to connect people to information and resources that will support her needs.

Gaps

A breakdown in communication or in the information chain can be crippling. Perhaps a whole menu item was dropped from the site due to software constraints, but no one told the designer. Or a required piece of content was forgotten during the initial project outline and now no one knows who's going to be writing, shooting, and editing the 10-minute video for the homepage. It happens. Think about

- The source of or reason for the gap, and whether it affects anything else

- Whether everyone knows what happened, not just those immediately affected

- Whether the project documentation has been amended to reflect the change

People

Not everyone will see the big picture. Sometimes people are so focused on trying to find a solution that they forget someone else solved a similar problem on a different project. Or sometimes two people are running into related problems, but are unaware of their parallel problems. Think about

- Who has the knowledge and resources to solve the problem in the best way

- Who's working on a task that directly affects other member of the team

- Whether any other teams within the organization have solved a similar problem, or launched a similar project

MANAGING ISN'T

Sending an email that reads, "See below" isn't going to bring people and solutions together. Be explicit and give people the information they need up front.

Observing vigilantly: Being the eyes and ears for the team

Once the project kicks off, it needs full-attention and watchfulness. This means being aware of what's happening in every facet of the project.

It also means pushing people—and the project. Not everyone will do everything right on the first try. And not everything will be up to standards after the first round. That's okay. But it's the project manager's job to see this and ensure everything gets up to par. Think about

- Whether technology is being leveraged to the best end

- Whether everyone is working to the best of their ability

- Whether the project needs to move in another direction to better fit the goals

Bottom line: If you're not doing each and every one of these things every day, then you're not project managing.

MANAGING ISN'T

Keeping an eye on things can look (and feel) like babysitting if done poorly. There will be people who need more follow-up than others. To avoid pandering to a bad habit, talk with the person about other ways that she can accomplish her tasks.

A successful project requires management in two directions: outward and inward.

Leadership looks outward: they build business, set the emotional energy of the organization, and establish expectations with clients and vendors. The project manager follows through on the promises being made out in the world—to the company's clients, to employees, and to anyone else.

See why project managers are kind of a big deal?!

YEAH, BUT…What if I don't have any control over the outward energy of the company?

GLAD YOU ASKED…Everyone represents their company at all times. All of your 'real life' behavior is actually a reflection of your company in some small way. Moreover, a project manager certainly has a lot of influence on energy levels, even if just within the team. But if the energy or tone that you're setting is drastically different than how things are typically done, have a meeting to set the tone and let the team know what to expect—and what you're going to expect from them.

The perfect project manager

Remember our orchestra metaphor? The project manager is like a conductor. She keeps the disparate groups working together so that the collective group completes the project simultaneously and successfully.

This central role requires a very particular kind of person, with distinct qualities.

Personable

The best project manager is likable. That might sound funny, but this is a job that's *all about* working with people. And people want to work with those they like and feel good about. It's a simple—but important—quality. If the team enjoys being around the project manager, trusts her, and has confidence in her, they'll do better work. And being able to connect and interact with her team makes it easier to communicate, collaborate, and motivate.

MEET THE TEAM: **Reacting to different types of people**

Every team has archetypal characters. Ultimately, you need these strong personality types to act productively and collaboratively within the team. Reacting to them intelligently makes all the difference. Here are two typical colleagues you'll likely encounter. You'll meet others in the following two chapters.

THE COMPLAINER. He always gets the job done, but likes to complain about every little thing along the way. While complaints are sometimes valid, this person simply enjoys the act of complaining.

The best response is to just listen. After complaining, he will likely move on and get everything done. But, remember to truly listen—sometimes among the litany of his complaints will lie a real issue. Don't let it pass you by.

THE HERO. This person is *really* good at a lot of things and has a tendency to swoop in, save the day, and fix all the problems that arise. This isn't always a good thing.

Watch carefully—the Hero goes into fix-it mode when he senses a vacuum or gap. If he jumps into a task that isn't his responsibility, question his reasons and make sure that it's the best thing *for the project* to have him doing it. If so, communicate what he's doing to the team so everyone knows. If not, encourage him to hand off the work to the right team member.

On the flip side, she has to enjoy interacting with and figuring out people. She doesn't have to be an extrovert, but she has to find people and their individual qualities interesting.

Determining what makes one person one way and another a different way is critical in motivating everyone to work well together. A project manager has to *want* to work *with* each person, not around them.

Imagine that people are like padlocks, and the right combination will unlock their potential. Of course, you can always open a padlock with a hammer. But that only works once—if you want to use that padlock again you're better off cracking the code. People work the same way—you can only hammer on them for so long before it stops working. The project manager will have better, longer-lasting results if she takes the time to figure people out.

Once that's done, a project manager has to figure out how to combine all the people and their personalities to the best effect. And then she has to tailor her own behavior to each.

Detail oriented

Project managers have to be the type of individuals that see, remember, and address the details. They're the people that capture everything and don't let anything fall through the cracks. The mind of the project manager must naturally be drawn to reviewing things, double-checking info, and trapping little details.

How individual project managers go about collecting and acting on all the details will, of course, be their own. But they have to be someone that has an inclination to do so.

Naturally communicative

A good project manager is someone who intuitively knows how to say something so that people *get* it. And how to tell if they didn't get it, so she can re-state it in a different, more understandable way.

Communicating isn't just what she says, it's also how she listens. If she absorbs information incorrectly and leads your team down the wrong path, she'll lose their respect. She must be comfortable asking questions and getting to the bottom of things, and be able to spot when someone may not be communicating effectively with her.

Actively online

It's crucial that interactive project managers are curious about technology and actively participate in it all the time. This means more than being on Facebook (though that's a start). It means reading about technology, learning about what's happening and what's being talked about in the industry, and tinkering with tech tools, like creating a new website for a friend or learning coding languages on the side.

The important point is to engage with technology. Because technology develops and changes so quickly and is so interconnected, no one in this industry can afford to learn only on the job.

Why does the project manager have to know this when she's not actually *doing* any of the technical things? Because she has to know how to ask questions, understand the big picture, and facilitate solutions with people that *are* dealing with technology. She doesn't have to *be* a programmer, but she must understand what programmers do. The same goes for design, front-end development, and quality assurance.

Takeaways

There you go. There's a lot to know about interactive project management and the people who do it. You can now consider yourself up to speed on

- The importance of the project manager's job and the crucial role that project managers play in the interactive project process.

- What project management entails: thinking, analyzing, communicating, and motivating. Rinse and repeat.

- The qualities needed to excel at and enjoy the job: being good with people, details, and communication, and a habit of living your life online, at least a lot of the time.

3

EMOTIONAL INTELLIGENCE

Technology doesn't drive projects, people do

If you want to do good work, you have to be able to motivate the people doing the work. The web is about people: they make it and they use it. Learning to work with the emotions that drive all people is key to a successful project.

In this chapter, we'll discuss

- What emotional intelligence is
- How to merge emotions and the workplace in a new professionalism
- Why emotional intelligence is important
- What emotional intelligence looks like in action
- Why caring is the bottom line

Emotions affect everything people do: every exchange, every conversation, every task—even in business. Think about it. The stock market rises and falls based on how investors *feel* about the market's stability; the consumer confidence index fluctuates based on the way people *feel* about the economy. These metrics that we think of as *business* are driven by *feelings*—some rational and fact-based and some not. Sometimes hard numbers say one thing, but a pervasive mood can override logic.

Because emotions drive actions, project managers have to figure out how to work with these emotions, not ignore them. It won't do much good to focus on a person's action without looking at the emotions that led him to do it. Emotions are not liabilities; they're assets. They mean we get excited, remain dedicated and loyal, and have creative ideas. But to effectively leverage these assets, we have to understand and manage them.

It used to be that a lot of the things that make us human—like feelings and personalities—were left at the door when we came to work. Well, they weren't *actually* left at the door, but they weren't acknowledged. We—the collective *we*—were focused on "professionalism." This meant not talking about our personal lives, not expressing our moods, and avoiding discussions about feelings or conflicts. (And many organizations still operate this way.) But here's the truth: Personal issues do affect work. Acknowledging that and reacting with basic human understanding goes a long way in making the whole team more productive. That's the new professionalism.

Let's get this out of the way: this isn't a "girl thing," it's a human thing. Both men and women show emotions at work. And emotional reactions don't always take the form of over-the-top dramatic behavior—in fact, that's not something to put up with. We're talking about normal, sometimes subtle, but still evident moments of being human. Mentally checking out, pacing, shouting, crying, leaving abruptly—these are all ways that people display emotions.

And being understanding doesn't mean being touchy-feely. The solution isn't a group hug. It's listening and guiding someone to the solution he needs. It's thinking about team members as humans.

What is emotional intelligence?

Emotional intelligence is the ability to manage and connect with people appropriately and effectively. It means being aware of—and managing—your own emotions, observing and responding to other people's emotional signals, and recognizing how to adjust to keep the energy focused and the project moving toward the goals at hand.

People with emotional intelligence

- Understand what others are feeling

- Are attuned to what's happening around them

- Connect with other people

- Recognize the nuances of language and nonverbal cues

- Facilitate and create productive energy

- Instill trust in the team

- Know how to work with their own strengths and weaknesses and those of others

Emotional intelligence can help make your exchanges with others healthy and productive, and foster healthy and productive exchanges among your entire team. It requires that you

- Notice how your own feelings affect you

- Leave your ego at the door

- Understand your place within an exchange

It results in

- Motivated people

- Strong relationships

- A better project

We all learned this stuff in kindergarten. Over time, we've just been trained to shut it off. We're here to reverse that. Let's not work so hard at avoiding and suppressing the emotions that will inevitably arise. Instead, let's work hard at managing them. Because happy people do good work.

The new professionalism

Business is about relationships. It always has been and always will be. And you don't want to do business with someone who makes you feel bad. Think about how you feel when you walk into a store and the employee looks irritated that you're there. Even if the store is selling exactly what you need, you might not buy it because you didn't *feel good* about the experience. Or, if you do buy it, you likely won't go back there again. Now imagine how important it is that people feel good about someone they're collaborating with over the duration of a three-, six- or twelve-month project. It's a big deal.

GET ALONG WITH OTHERS. What are we to do with all this human stuff? React like a human! Listen, watch, talk, ask questions, and observe. Sounds pretty basic, doesn't it? It is. It's like almost every relationship we conduct outside work.

CONNECT WITH PEOPLE ON A PERSONAL LEVEL. This doesn't mean getting personal *per se*. It means talking to them like they're people. It's asking them if they understand, or reading their faces to see that they clearly don't. It's making sure that people have what they need to get their work done. It's asking how you can help when you can tell they need support.

TREAT ADULTS LIKE ADULTS. As a leader, this means not making ridiculous rules that make people feel like they're in grade school. And not requiring people to do superfluous tasks just to prove they're paying attention. Assume that your colleagues are adults and then treat them as such. In the end, if they're doing good work and getting it done on time, does it really matter if they came in at 9:00 a.m. or 9:34 a.m.? Probably not.

FOSTER A SUPPORTIVE ENVIRONMENT. Clients and colleagues will all have questions, concerns, ideas, and problems. Every person on a team is responsible for creating an environment in which others feel comfortable expressing all of these. Not just the good stuff.

MEET THE TEAM: **Reacting to different types of people**

Here are a few more archetypal characters that you'll find on your team; others can be found in Chapter 2, "Interactive Project Management 101" and Chapter 4, "Communication." They're strong personality types that, ultimately, need to work collaboratively within the team to keep things moving along. Reacting to them intelligently makes all the difference.

THE TIME BOMB. They have limits, and when those limits are reached, there's a big reaction— as in, a slow buildup that leads to a meltdown.

Learn to read the cues. All time bombs will give cues, but they're subtle.

THE WILD CARD. They're unpredictable. If they have ten tasks to do, they'll do eight with spot-on precision and the other two completely off base. And you'll never know which two these will be. The danger is pretty clear: Something could go wrong, and it's hard to know what it will be.

Keep a close eye on their daily statuses and have frequent check-in conversations; there'll probably be cues for you to read.

THE LONER. This person wants to do everything alone. That's not to say he's hard to work with, he's just not a natural group person. Some loners just don't think well "in public." They need to be alone to process their thoughts.

Respect that, but don't let them do too much on their own or they risk getting out of sync with the rest of the group.

Why is emotional intelligence important?

There's a laundry list of reasons why emotional intelligence is valuable and important within the workplace, but here's the big one: It will—without a doubt—lead to a better project.

It's the people within any process that make it successful. Happy people do good work, remember? As Daniel Pink explains in his book *Drive: The Surprising Truth About What Motivates Us*—people are motivated by autonomy, mastery, and purpose.[1] Those three things make people feel good about where they're at, what they're contributing, and why. Emotional intelligence is required to gauge whether people around you are feeling these things. It's also required to determine if *you're* feeling those things.

Moreover, people are unpredictable. This doesn't mean we're all ticking time bombs, it just means that we can't always know how people will act. Unlike a printer with a paper jam, a person with a problem can't be fixed with a few rote steps. You actually have to engage with a person, and adjust your response to the situation. Clearly, that's where emotional intelligence comes in.

Emotional intelligence in action

There can be a tricky dynamic between those who are in the interactive industry and those who aren't. To make it all work, the interactive team must accomplish two broad tasks when it comes to connecting with clients: Earn trust and manage expectations. Sometimes clients need a one-on-one chat about the project's progress; sometimes they need data and evidence of how things are going.

Similarly, when it comes to an internal team, two goals are front and center: managing and motivating people. That's the only way a project will get done well. Yep, it always comes back to the people. It always comes back to emotional itelligence. What does this look like in action?

Don't get defensive: Understand what others are feeling

Think about the situation from the other person's perspective.

WITH CLIENTS. Often clients want something for a ridiculously cheap price, or ask why it takes so much time to build something. Maybe they really don't know or maybe they're just being human (don't we all want to have our cake and eat it too?). Either way, they won't hear the answer if your team responds aggressively. Listen to them to determine the exact things that they are

---

1 Daniel Pink, *Drive: The Surprising Truth About What Motivates Us* (Riverhead Trade, 2009).

confused or alarmed by. Then respond and explain, neutrally. This will make things clearer for them and for you (you'll start to learn more about their concerns). And more open dialogue leads, inevitably, to more trust.

WITH INTERNAL TEAMS. No one responds well to defensiveness. It leads to finger pointing, blame, and divisiveness. Assess what they're thinking and feeling. Don't respond with something like, "Well, *you* didn't do..." By putting yourself in their shoes (look, there's your ego walking out the door) you can better address their issue.

Manage meetings: Be sensitive to what's happening around you

Talk about a PR problem! People hate meetings so much that some companies have tried to ban them. Meetings aren't the problem: the people running them are. Meetings are important events. They're where people come face-to-face, where many decisions get made, and where details are explained. But for all of that to happen a person has to effectively manage the meeting. As a project manager, actively manage meetings—the people, the topics, and the energy. As team members and clients, don't tolerate sloppy meetings. Problem solved.

WITH CLIENTS. Some meetings require a very specific feel and finesse— maybe the client needs high energy or maybe they need to talk to the developer about all the technology details. Every client will need a unique set of people and perspectives to feel comfortable with the team. Doing this correctly shows that you're considering *what the client needs* and executing the project responsibly.

Never send only one person to a meeting. No one person will ever get along with everyone. More than one person—when it's the *right* people—will increase the opportunity for connection with the client. Moreover, multiple people mean multiple perspectives on the client, their needs, and their personalities.

That being said, not everyone needs to go to meetings! Too many people in a room can make things uncomfortable. If a team member isn't going to resonate with the client, it will be noticed. If no one understands why a person is there, it will be obvious. And that isn't good for the relationship, or the vibe in the room.

CHOOSE WISELY

Who should go to meetings—and who shouldn't—is a gray area. Knowing the answer to this question, for each meeting, is the mark of an excellent project manager. The only way to get good at this is to practice. Observe what happens with different people in the room, and how they react to the way you manage the agenda.

WITH INTERNAL TEAMS. Don't waste people's time. Find the balance between keeping everyone in the loop and not making them attend meetings that pull them away from their work unnecessarily.

Set the tone for the team. The whole team is responsible for being excited about every project. Even in the midst of problems and setbacks—which are inevitable—set a productive tone. It might be "down to business" or "Go, team!" (skip the pom-poms). Pay attention to the communication and energy you're getting from your team. They'll tell you—in words or actions—what's needed to keep the project on track.

Establish expectations: Facilitate and create productive energy

Establishing expectations provides a sense of calm because people have an idea of what's going to happen, how it's going to happen, and who's doing what.

WITH CLIENTS. Every relationship benefits from clear expectations, even ones with clients. Or perhaps, *especially* ones with clients. This should start early, like in the pitch. Tell them exactly what they can and cannot expect from your internal team.

Be proactive and frame the discussion so that clients understand exactly what the expectations are ("Yes, we really do need a weekly status meeting" or "No, you can't email us 14 times a day and expect an immediate response to each one"). Also make the intentions behind the expectations clear (efficiency, cost-effectiveness, sanity); it builds trust with clients. Earn trust *and* manage expectations all at once? Perfect.

WITH INTERNAL TEAMS. Establishing what is expected of your team keeps everyone feeling like they're in control of their own work. When it comes down to it, most people want to know what they're supposed to do, when they're supposed to do it, and who's doing the other stuff. It's hard for anyone to feel like they've got a handle on things if unexpected tasks or deadlines are constantly thrown at them. Sure, this happens occasionally, that's life. But letting your internal team know as much as possible empowers (and motivates) them to invest in their roles and responsibilities.

Be trustworthy: Share your values and keep your promises

Understanding your company's values is key to connecting with clients and your internal team. If they trust that you know this, and you follow through with it, they'll feel that much better about your relationship.

WITH CLIENTS. As you get to know clients and their businesses, they get to know you, too. During this process you have the opportunity to make promises and share the values that guide the team's work. Once this is done, you have to follow through.

At Clockwork, we commit to managing projects that are delivered on time and on budget. And we do. This sometimes means having tough conversations that emphasize realistic expectations about budget and schedules and discussions about expanding these when it's necessary. But, we have a responsibility to have those conversations because they allow us to keep our promises. And with every promise we keep we add to the trusting relationship we've built with the client.

WITH INTERNAL TEAMS. Companies and leaders not only make promises to clients, they also make promises to staff. And vice versa. On the individual or company level, be who and what you say you are. Walk the walk. Everything works better when people trust the people they're working with, whether you're the boss or not.

Acknowledge expertise: Know how to work with people's strengths and weaknesses

Recognizing and leveraging everyone's skills and knowledge will get the best work from people, which will lead to the best project.

WITH CLIENTS. Acknowledge the smarts, the vision, and the know-how that clients bring to the project. They may not know software or technology (or they might), but they know their business. That's what they bring to your collaborative table. And that's a pretty big thing.

By empowering them to own their expertise, you're showing them the collaborative nature of interactive projects. Our job is to realize clients' visions. It's to translate their business and their objectives into digital media. It isn't to tell them what to do.

> Many clients feel disempowered when it comes to interactive projects and say things like, "Well, you guys know best!" Remind them that their knowledge of their industry and their business is invaluable and their participation is critical.

WITH INTERNAL TEAMS. Every person on the team is important. Period. The project will get done only if everyone participates. Emphasizing this within the internal team will give individuals a sense of mastery and ownership over their roles and tasks. While a designer might have feedback or insight for a developer, ultimately it should be the developer's responsibility to make development decisions. And vice versa. Encourage this behavior in your team.

Read a room: Recognize the nuances of language and nonverbal cues

People say things a million different ways. And only one tenth of the ways include direct, precise language. We're human, what do you expect?

WITH CLIENTS. The constant goal with clients is to minimize—if not eliminate—miscommunication. Most people don't raise their hand and say, "I don't understand what you're saying." It would be awesome if they did. Instead, they usually do something like furrow their eyebrows, or look at their colleagues to see if *they* seem to get it, or say, "Hmmm," or stop paying attention altogether. Everyone on your internal team needs to pay attention to these subtle cues. They signal that what you *think* is happening may not actually be happening.

It's important to gauge if the clients seem happy and comfortable with your team, or if there's some underlying dissatisfaction with how the project is turning out. Sometimes you have no idea what the problem is, but you can tell something is not quite right based on subtle cues. Talk to the clients about it to see if they can help you determine the problem.

ASK, DON'T ASSUME

If you pick up on a facial expression or feeling, ask the person if it means anything.

WITH INTERNAL TEAMS. Whether your team is gathering for a meeting, a working session, or just hanging out, pay attention to what's happening. There are always other things going on in their workday or in their minds. There are other projects, ups and downs in their personal lives, interoffice dynamics, and more. It's the project manager's responsibility to watch the team to ensure that these distractions aren't negatively affecting the project. Is there someone who's disengaged? Is there someone who's not doing his work? Is there a team member who's afraid to admit that he doesn't know how to do something, and will the client end up paying for this mistake? Here's the thing, though: none of the cues that people give off will be verbal. It'll be on their faces, in their posture, in their eye contact, or maybe in their tone of voice. The key is to watch and listen. Very carefully.

When you see (or hear) this kind of behavior, you have to call this out—not in the meeting or in front of people, but separately. And connect them with people or information that will support them. Find out *why* it's happening (the source), and act on that, rather than acting on *what's* happening (the symptom).

If you're *not* the project manager, you can *also* do this. If someone is dropping the ball or his work seems compromised, talk to him. See what's happening—not confrontationally, but as a friend.

> It's tempting to think that other people's issues are "not my problem." But, people who are negative or disengaged have a disastrous effect on the quality of your project, and on the mood of the rest of the team. If you're trying to deliver an awesome product and you have unhappy team members—it's definitely your problem.

Enable people: Connect with and hear your team

Everyone has tasks and responsibilities on a project. It's important that everyone on the team—and especially the project manager—makes sure conditions are conducive to actually getting the work done.

WITH CLIENTS. Try to determine what will help clients complete their tasks. Ask them directly or reach out and suggest some ways to tackle the to-dos. You might need to send them reminders about meetings and due dates for feedback. You might have to give them a checklist of what they are reviewing in each document. Work closely with them to find a way to be productive.

WITH INTERNAL TEAMS. This will look different in *every* situation. There is no predetermined set of actions that will enable your team members to do their best work. But there are general conditions that will create an environment in which good work can be done:

- Give them a voice and listen to it, then help them manage their time and space.

- Be compassionate, empathetic, and understanding.

- Don't be afraid to lay down the law and give them a kick in the pants.

All of these conditions can be facilitated by talking to your team members. Ask them how they're doing; see if they're frazzled, see if they're happy. Hear what they have to say. These simple interactions can go surprisingly far in creating a productive workspace. And if you see red flags or possible problems, you can track them or take action immediately. Get the information you need to ensure things are moving along, while the team feels connected and heard.

YOU'RE NOT MY BOSS

Team members will have bosses and managers outside the project. As the project manager within a project, be sure you're acting appropriately within the hierarchy of your organization, and escalating issues if necessary.

Apathy is the enemy of awesome

The bottom line is this: Care about the people you're working with. As the project manager, you should want to support the people around you, and the entire internal team should want to make the clients happier than they ever imagined.

If everyone cares about each other's overall well-being and the well-being of the project, there is a far greater chance that innovation, problem solving, and creativity will emerge. The people—your team, the clients, and *you*—are your users. If you care about the end user of a website, you should also care about the end users of your energy and actions.

> **YEAH BUT**…*What if I really don't care about the people I work with, or the work we're doing? Or what if it's clear that my company doesn't care about me?*

> **GLAD YOU ASKED**…*You need to find a new job.*

Takeaways

Emotions factor into everything we do, both in and out of the workplace. That's why it's worth it to get intelligent about working *with* emotions, not against them.

- Emotional intelligence is about effectively managing your relationships with others and connecting with people.

- The place for emotions in the workplace is in how you engage and respond; get along, be personal, treat everyone like the adults they are, and support your team.

- Emotional intelligence is important because it means better business.

- In action, emotional intelligence looks like the kind of interacting we do with a lot of people in our lives—talking, caring, listening, being open. Now it's time to apply these natural tendencies to our professional relationships.

4

COMMUNICATION

Right message. Right medium. Right time.

There are countless ways to communicate with team members and stakeholders, from email and documents to meetings and calls. An effective project manager wrangles all that *can* be said in *any number of ways* into what *needs* to be said and delivers it in the *best way possible*.

In this chapter, we'll discuss

- What good communication looks like
- The common types of communication and what they're good for
- Best practices

All projects require communication. What's different about interactive projects? There's a wide range of personalities and stakeholders involved—from the IE6-hating developer to the executive requesting "the next Facebook." Not only that, there are opinions, requirements, restrictions, and requests coming from all of them.

All of this causes tension. Effective communication is the key to preventing and resolving the tension and misunderstandings that arise.

Using emotional intelligence to understand your team is just the beginning. Applying those observations and experiences using communication is pivotal to facilitating productive and collaborative engagement among your team.

What does good communication look like?

IT GOES TWO WAYS

Project managers are responsible for communicating clearly *and* facilitating good communication among the other team members. Watch out for possible miscommunication as email exchanges and conversations happen.

USE A COMMON LANGUAGE

There's marketing speak, tech speak, admin speak, industry speak, and more, plus a million dialects of each. There are many ways that stakeholders talk about problems, solutions, and everything in between. Always think about how to speak in jargon-free terms.

Practicing good communication, at every opportunity, will make a huge difference on any project. Transferring information, exchanging ideas, providing explanations, and achieving goals all rest on effective communication. As project manager, you set the stage by ensuring that communication has the following four qualities:

OPEN. Being honest about expectations, objectives, and restrictions is one of the most crucial elements of successful communication. You might have to ask a lot of questions to get a client to be open, or maybe you'll have to reiterate the value of openness to your team. Bring back-channel conversations to the forefront and stress to your team that openness strengthens the project.

CLEAR. Understand what's going on with your team and the client. And make sure they understand, too. Listen, ask questions, process, and think through what they're saying. And confirm understanding with others, both clients and the internal team.

COLLABORATIVE. Collaboration requires productive, two-way communication. Both you and the client bring expertise and value to the project. They know their business; you know yours. Together you make something great. Don't try to make your client feel like you know everything about everything, because you don't—and neither does your team, your department, or your organization. And make sure that your client doesn't treat you or your organization like vendors. Your team does more than simply execute clients' ideas; it brings value and insight, an asset that your client must recognize if you're going to work collaboratively.

THOROUGH. Communication is an invaluable tool in properly documenting and recording the life cycle of a project. Capturing the thinking and talking that happens apart from forms and documents is important in establishing a shared understanding among the team. Recognizing that a project is veering off course requires thoroughness: Read carefully, ask questions, call out red flags, and then document and communicate the changes.

The effects of good communication extend beyond the project and into the life of the product. Think about this when managing a project. From beginning to (no) end, effective communication will mean success beyond the launch date.

REVISIT DOCUMENTATION

Check meeting notes, scratch paper, or any place where you might have jotted down a task, decision, or requirement. Make sure that critical information gets transferred from temporary notes to more permanent documentation.

Setting the stage for success

Prepare the team for the kind of communication that will arise and the potential problems that communication can solve.

Welcome candid conversations

Not all news can be butterflies and rainbows. Realistically, we have to have conversations that are loaded with stress, bad news, or complex information.

Collaborating effectively with clients means tackling tough conversations. Project partnerships have to start with an early acknowledgement that these will occur and an agreement that they will be processed together. This has to go all the way to the top of the organization. As an executive or leader, it's important to welcome these moments as an integral part of the process, not as a failure of the team.

Prevent misunderstandings

Technology creates tension. (Think about it until you agree.[1]) This is one of the primary differences between interactive projects and any other type of project. But you can alleviate some of this tension if the *reasons* for it are addressed with open communication.

Openly discuss the truths about technology. This will give clients the context and knowledge they need to understand what makes interactive projects different. Here are three points that prep the team for what's ahead:

---

1 Mahtab Rezai, Twitter, 2009.

TECHNOLOGY ALWAYS EVOLVES. Many clients are still more comfortable with traditional media. An ad campaign or a rebranding effort has a finite end, but interactive projects are different. They're always changing: existing software is updated, new software is created, and this affects how it all works together. If you can help clients understand and anticipate this it empowers them to think in evolutionary terms. It's no one's fault if a new browser is introduced the day the project launches. It's just how the interactive world works.

THE LAUNCH IS THE BEGINNING, NOT THE END. It's very satisfying to launch a site or an app, and it's certainly well worth celebrating, but not because it's the end of the project or the work. Most interactive projects need to evolve. They'll require updates to content, site architecture, code, or software. It's like a puppy: To keep it alive you have to feed it and walk it, and it sometimes poops on the floor. Making the client aware of this and keeping it in the front of their minds will give them a better sense of the real scope of the project beyond the launch day balloon-drop.

SET REALISTIC EXPECTATIONS. Recognizing and tempering unrealistic expectations will keep everyone happier in the long run. Technology won't solve everyone's problems; it may not eliminate work. Discussing this proactively *before* it's a problem makes it easier to correct if it *becomes* a problem.

Types of communication

Understanding why and when to communicate with the team is critical to doing it effectively.

Transactional vs. relational

The purpose of project communication can be broadly categorized by two intentions: to exchange information (transactional) or to build relationships (relational). Knowing which category your information falls into will determine which mode you use to communicate it (Figure 4.1).

> *YEAH, BUT…How can I execute relational communication if I don't have access to the client?*

GLAD YOU ASKED...If you're in an organization where project managers can't connect with the client directly, contact the account manager with the same messages you would send the client. From there, suggest that you both reach out—or just the account manager, if that's more appropriate for your workplace.

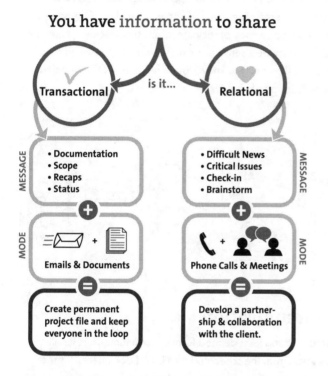

You have information to share

FIGURE 4.1
The differences between transactional and relational communication and common scenarios in which to use each.

Scheduled communication

Scheduled communication could be daily, weekly, biweekly, and in the form of email, meetings, and so on.

The most common example of scheduled communication is the status report. Make a schedule for disseminating the status report and stick to it. Also, establish what the report's content will be and stick to that, too. For example, weekly status emails might be sent on Wednesdays to all stakeholders. The emails could include what was accomplished the previous week, what is currently being worked on, and what is slated for the following week. (Look for guidelines for kick-ass status reports later in this chapter.)

Who gets status emails? Everyone. Yes, everyone. Not just clients and/or decision makers. Everyone should be in the loop and on the same page. Think back to those four attributes we talked about: open, clear, collaborative, and thorough. These group emails will help keep the project working within these lines.

Establishing regular communication will also help organize the stakeholders—both internal and external (Figure 4.2). People can be loosely grouped into three types based on how they participate: discussers, deciders, and communicators. This will also create a sense of calm. Everyone knows when they'll find out the details that they need to know. And it helps avoid the dreaded, "Where is this?" emails from stakeholders.

FIGURE 4.2
As the client and your team determines the discussers, deciders, and communicators on each team, the chain of communication starts to look more organized and efficient.

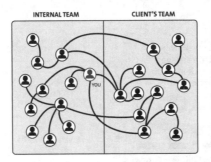 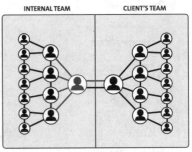

CHECK IN

If a client or colleague expects an immediate response, you can always reply with, "I'm working on this. I'll let you know by the end of the day." This let's them know you are acting on their request, without pressuring you to come up with a definitive reply in minutes.

Ad hoc communication

This is the most frequent and least defined form of communication. It's all the stuff that happens apart from the scheduled emails and documents. It's the random emails, impromptu phone calls, handwritten notes, or feedback. Let's face it: This is the most typical kind of correspondence that happens during a project. And it can also be the most difficult to wrangle.

Most clients won't be as organized as you want them to be with their communication. Most of your designers and developers won't be, either. They'll pepper you with rapid-fire emails with ideas, changes, or questions. Sometimes, they'll shoot you *many* of these a day. Or their feedback will be something really clear, like, "Can you change this? It doesn't seem right."

How to handle this

Being aware of what you may be communicating nonverbally is as important as creating a good paper trail. Poise and calm will have a huge impact on the morale and outlook of the team.

TAKE YOUR TIME. Don't let questions coming at you with lightning speed throw you off. Responding within 10 minutes of every email doesn't mean you're better. The quality of the response is far more important than the speed of the response.

Clients look to interactive teams for insight and knowledge. Give them that. Not surprisingly, sometimes insight and knowledge take longer than 10 minutes. Nearly every question leads to a few more due to the interconnectivity of inter-active projects. Proactively analyzing what potential follow-up questions may be or what aspects of the project the original question affects takes time.

BE CALM. As you find out information or details that make you feel like your project is going off-course, stay levelheaded, at least in front of your team. Even if you never say, "How the hell are we going to get this done?!" the team will see it on your face if you're not careful.

RIGHT TIME AND PLACE

If you want or need to freak out—we all do sometimes—do it out of sight of your project team and in the company of someone who can help you brainstorm solutions or just be a sounding board.

MEET THE TEAM: Reacting to different types of people

Here are the remaining archetypal characters that you'll find on your team. (Others appear in Chapter 2, "Interactive Project Management 101" and Chapter 3, "Emotional Intelligence.") They're strong personality types that, ultimately, need to work collaboratively within the team to keep things moving along. Reacting to them intelligently makes all the difference.

THE BLOWHARD. She gets riled up. She makes exclamations. She blows off steam—not really complaints, just big, blustery energy. But like the complainer, she puts her head down and works when it comes down to it. The danger is that this high-energy spouting off might make others feel uncomfortable or taken aback or even attacked.

This person will probably always need to vent, but encouraging her to do it in a private, con-trolled environment is a good idea.

THE GEM. This person is exactly what you think: a fantastic colleague, great at her job, totally reli-able. Thank your lucky stars if you get one or more than one of these on your team. Cherish her.

Hope for one of these on every team. Just be careful that she doesn't slide into Hero territory.

Best practices

Communication is broad and can mean many things. Following a few guidelines will make it manageable and effective.

Hit send with success

Effective formatting can mean the difference between clarity and confusion, but people don't do it, as evidenced by our inboxes. People hate emails so much that some companies are trying to ban it. Email isn't the problem, sending bad emails is. The bottom line: Don't make people work hard for information.

BREAK UP LONG EMAILS. When you're writing a long email, break it up into sections. Start with a summary that concisely outlines the main idea(s) and any action items within the email. Follow this with the details. This way the reader can grasp the key info quickly, and then read the details only if she has to.

TYPOS MATTER

Every time you send an email, you have the opportunity to help or hurt your credibility. Typos aren't about the grammar police. They matter because they affect peoples' trust in you: if people can't trust you with small things, it's harder to trust you with big things.

PUT COMPLICATED EMAILS IN A PHONE CALL SANDWICH. With interactive projects, sometimes you have to convey complex or technical information. Here's what to do:

- Write the email (check the long email tip above!), but don't send it.

- Call the client and give her a heads up that a long or complicated email is coming her way. Don't make it sound ominous: The point is to prevent fear and glazed-over eyes. Say something like, "I'm about to send you a really detailed email. It has a lot of information in it that I've tried to organize into digestible parts, but here's the basic summary. I will call you in a bit to see if you have any questions about it."

- Send the email.

- Later, call the client for follow-up. Make sure she understands everything in the email and is prepared to deal with whatever might be required.

DON'T THROW GRENADES. Never send an email that states a problem with no solution. Be complete: state the issue. Then, make suggestions about how to correct the issue. List some next steps that the client needs to or should take, or invite her suggestions on how to solve the problem.

FORMATTING IS YOUR FRIEND. Use things like subheads, bullet points, and bold text to make the information as easy to read as possible. (Side note: This is one of those things that clients love and developers hate. Some of them may even have their email set up to strip out certain types of formatting.)

CALL OUT NAMES. Get people's attention if you need it. When information is directed at a particular person, add her name or a special callout in front of the pertinent info or question. Highlight or bold names so team members can easily scan long emails for their callouts. Whatever tool you use is up to you, but make it easy for everyone to spot with just a scan.

Keep everyone in the loop all the time

At Clockwork, we use two email aliases—internal and external—that team members use to communicate with the project teams. The internal alias goes to all internal team members; the external one goes to everyone on the internal team as well as all client stakeholders. Almost all correspondence goes through the group alias. This terrifies some people, and shocks others. This is a radical departure from the way project correspondence happens almost everywhere else, across industries.

What is an email alias?

An email alias as we use it at Clockwork is a singular email address that has multiple recipients. For example, when someone emails internal_bestprojectever@company.com or bestprojectever@company.com, it goes to the entire internal or external teams, respectively, working on the project. Figure 4.3 shows examples of information sent through an alias.

WRITE THE SUMMARY LAST

Sometimes you won't know how to summarize what you're writing until you've finished it. When writing a long email, get all your thoughts out first. Then, go back. Reorganize, edit, reformat, and, as a final step, write the executive summary.

KEEP IT CLEAR

Be sure to label the internal alias with the word "internal" first, or you risk sending internal conversations to the client too easily.

FIGURE 4.3
A selection of the types of information and conversations that should ultimately be routed through the project email alias. The goal is to keep everyone on the project aware of decisions, conversations, and updates.

**DIY
ALIAS**

Making an alias does require some handy IT department work. If this isn't possible, create a contact list in your own email program for internal and all project recipients. That way it's easy and quick for you to email everyone.

**ASK
YOURSELF**

Don't know when you— or others—are hoarding? Here's a hypothetical question that may clarify things: If you got hit by a bus, would someone be able to come in and understand the work you did and are doing on a project? If not, you're hoarding.

Why use an email alias?

IT KEEPS EVERYONE ON THE SAME PAGE. All stakeholders deserve to see *what's* being said and how it's being said. This allows the project manager to focus on macro tasks, like hierarchizing and prioritizing information, rather than trafficking information. Everyone can be confident that critical information will be passed along to the right people, but they are still aware of what's going on.

IT REDUCES THE TELEPHONE EFFECT. Remember that game? A phrase is whispered to one person, they whisper it to another person, and so on, all around a circle. Then the last person says the phrase *she* heard out loud. Every single time it will be different from the original phrase. That's super funny on the school playground in third grade, but slightly less funny when it's critical information about a client's project and your job depends on it.

IT GIVES PEOPLE PERMISSION TO IGNORE EMAILS. Another effect of group aliases is counterintuitive to what people expect. A common response to us describing the email alias is: "You must be overwhelmed by emails!" Actually, the opposite is true: It gives everyone permission to read them (or not) at will. This sounds like a bad thing, but it's not. As people receive the emails, they are tangentially aware of the conversations, yet they know that if something is needed it will be called out by the project manager (by using a callout technique like we discussed above).

IT IMPROVES THE END PRODUCT. Interactive projects have many stakeholders that all see different risks, forecast different outcomes, and bring different ideas to the table. Allowing everyone to see all correspondence leads to more eyes and minds considering all aspects of the project and increases everyone's investment in the project. That's priceless.

IT REDUCES HOARDING. Somehow, somewhere, people got the idea that if they're the keeper of information, they'll be totally indispensable and will have eternal job security. This just isn't true. No one likes a hoarder. It makes everyone's job harder. If someone has to work at getting information to do their job, they are taking valuable time away from actually *doing* their job.

Figure 4.4 shows how the email alias relates to communicators, deciders, and discussers.

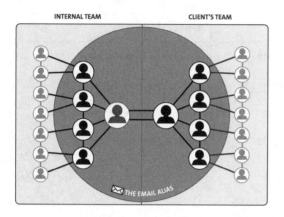

FIGURE 4.4
The primary communicators on each team—internal and client side—send the majority of the email communication through the alias. The deciders receive every message to stay up-to-date, and can certainly contribute as necessary.

Be consistent and clear with scheduled communication

People respond well to predictability, openness, and clarity. When you're communicating use tools that adhere to those standards. Think of this communication as a snapshot. It should give just enough information to be useful and explanatory, and never so much information that key details become lost like a needle in a haystack.

Forms and documents

CREATE TITLES AND HEADLINES. Make the contents and the purpose of the form visible at a glance.

MAKE IT EASY TO SEE WHAT NEEDS TO HAPPEN. Does the form require a signature? Make it clear. Does the form require an answer? Make it clear.

MAKE THEM EASY TO PRINT. Make sure the contents fit easily onto a standard sheet of paper. Make sure it doesn't contain an embedded image that's huge and will clog up the printer queue.

CREATE A CHANGE LOG. This will make it easy for the client, and you, to track the files. At a quick glance, you'll know if you're reading the most up-to-date version and what changes have been made.

DON'T HIT DELETE

If you're deleting something that was initially very important, use the strikethrough formatting tool rather than actually deleting it. This allows the team to still see it and easily note that it's been "removed" from consideration. It's a clearer way to communicate that the project changed course and easier to track later, if you're retracing your steps.

Revision	Date	Notes/Author Initials
.01	1/31/2012	Draft for internal review [MCW]
.02	2/15/2012	Draft for client review [NEL]
.03	3/2/2012	Revised draft for review/approval [ECN]
1.0	3/20/2012	Baseline approval [MCW]

Status reports

USE A CONSISTENT FORMAT. Always have the information in the same order, use the same callout techniques, and make it easy to print.

USE UNDERSTANDABLE LANGUAGE. This isn't the place to use a lot of jargon (is there ever a place for that?). Use language and terms that are familiar to everyone who reads it.

COVER EVERYTHING. Don't leave anything out. The clients should be getting all the information they need in this communication. They should come to rely on it and see it as the official progress report. If you leave the bad or tough news out, it will become apparent.

BE RESPECTFUL. Be firm and clear, but don't be a jerk. If something changed direction, don't let on that it was annoying, even if it was. Collaboration won't happen if anyone on the team starts feeling antagonized or attacked.

Wrangle, then react with ad hoc communication

Project managers control and disseminate everything that needs to be communicated. This means that they also have a lot of information coming *at* them. Organize your communication for optimal effect: Digestible, thoughtful communication helps people—and their brains—do their jobs well.

How to handle this

COLLECT AND ORGANIZE THE INFORMATION. Do this in whatever way makes sense for your project or the correspondence: by type—ideas, action items, red flags, decisions—or by affected stakeholders—client, writers, developers, executives. Make the information make sense to you, and then add the details that will make it make sense to others.

DETERMINE HOW TO COMMUNICATE. We're used to email. That's pretty much the go-to form of communication these days. But it should primarily be used for transactional aspects of a project. At times, it's best to reach out in person, for that relational approach. This doesn't necessarily mean face-to-face, but it does mean a real conversation in real time.

Here are some situations when it's best to have a conversation:

- If there's a high chance that something will be misconstrued or misinterpreted in writing: "As we mentioned earlier" can sound like "We told you so" with the wrong intonation.

- If it's a difficult message: "About that launch date…"

- If it's a complicated issue that requires explanation.

- If you feel like you should connect with your client. Follow your gut on this one. If it's been a while and you think that reestablishing a real connection—not just an electronic one—sounds right, do it.

DISTRIBUTE THE INFORMATION. Take the organized information and disseminate it. Part of it may go in an email to your team; part of it may go into a document that is then sent for reapproval from the client; part of it may have already been addressed in a phone call. The key is to make it easy to read, understand, and respond to. That's one of the key responsibilities of the project manager: to make sense of things and communicate this "sense" to the client and internal teams.

Follow-up after phone calls and meetings

When you have a phone conversation or meeting, follow up with an email that summarizes what was covered. It doesn't have to be an Official Recap of the Conversation form, just an email that references the discussion and quickly sums up the points. This accomplishes three things:

- It relays the conversation to the whole team (use the alias!).

- It provides a record for everyone (in some circles this is known as CYA—cover your, well, you know).

- It helps ensure that whatever points were talked about were actually *understood*.

Killing three birds with one, simple stone. Sorry, birds.

These are all important accomplishments, but the last point—making sure it was understood—is a critical, client-facing detail. Miscommunication happens. People say one thing, but mean something else; you hear one thing, they meant another. Really, it doesn't matter how it happens; you want to prevent it.

This recap gives all parties a chance to see *in writing* what was heard and what action is being taken. If there's a discrepancy between what was meant and what was understood, that will become clear right away, as opposed to later, *after* action was taken.

Deliver context, not truth bombs

Truth bombs are brutal facts without context. Problems, issues, and dilemmas happen. How you convey them can make all the difference in the world to you and your client, and your relationship.

Look at your communication with this in mind. You can recognize when you are about to send a truth bomb. Remember, something that seems straightforward to you can be very scary to people who don't have enough info or tech knowledge to provide a context or meaning on their own.

THINK ABOUT: Translating a truth bomb

The Problem: A popular Internet browser just released a new version and parts of a client's site won't work with it. (Surprise!)

Truth bomb: An email that says, "Your site is broken." (I'm sure you think we're joking, but we've seen emails like this.)

Context: An in-person conversation starting with, "The browser came out with a new version, which they do every so often, and we're noticing that some elements aren't working like we intended. We'll do some testing on our side and let you know what we find. Then we can determine what you'll need to do to bring your site up to date."

Give a solution-focused no

We all want to give clients what they want. But here's the problem: What they want isn't always what they need. If what they're asking for seems (or definitely is) a bad idea, tell them. Here's where it gets a little tricky.

Even if the answer is no, it's never *just* no because that doesn't help reach a solution. That doesn't mean that we do everything we're asked. Far from it. But we make a lot of effort to avoid stopping at the word *no*.

Being honest about whether something is possible, logical, or neither—all without just saying no—requires finessing.

PUT A POSITIVE SPIN ON THE NEGATIVE MESSAGE. When people hear no, they react a certain way—they close down and get defensive, and may become even more entrenched in their perspective. Ultimately, no matter what you're saying no to or disagreeing with, you need them to collaborate on a solution. Couching your "no" within positivity and productiveness paves the path toward collaboration. For example, you might say, "I see what you mean and what you're going for. Another way to achieve that might be _____. Leading questions can get to the root goal or intention, which you can then solve another way.

FIGURE OUT HOW TO SUPPORT THE ARGUMENT. Each client has different concerns and objectives. Some will repsond to an argument about technology restrictions, whereas others may respond to aesthetics. Some won't really respond to either. Given your experience with them, choose a persuasive path.

USE REASON AND LOGIC. Don't ever just state your critique or opinion of their solution without giving real reasons and using sound logic. "Because we think it's best" doesn't count. You have to give them evidence, whether that's usability stats, development restrictions, or something else.

RULE OF THREE

Like in comedy, we apply the rule of three. Voice your solution-focused "no" three times, then drop it. After three times it's pestering. As long as you can—with a clear conscience—launch the project the way the client is asking, let it go. Perhaps later, they'll see your point. Perhaps not. Sometimes that's just how it goes.

Good news and bad news at the same velocity

"Good news and bad news at the same velocity" is one of our key company values.[2] It's a promise that you make with your team to get the best end product every time. When you uphold this, what you're really saying is, "We will always tell you what you need to know about a project."

---

2 We have to give Gary Clark credit for this valuable principle. It's served us well.

Negative feedback is a lot easier to hear—*really* hear—if the recipient knows it's coming from a shared value. With a team relationship based on trust and understanding, constructive criticism is welcomed because it means that the project will be improved upon and, ultimately, better.

Diffuse tension with four words

Every time you talk to anyone about anything—so yes, all the time—you carry the emotions of the message with you. And the person to whom you're talking responds to those emotions. For example, if you're telling someone that you just won a $20 million lotto, maybe you'd jump up and down or smile like a kid in a candy store. And when they hear the news, they'd get wide-eyed and put on a happy face, too.

When you have difficult messages—be it bad news, problems, complications, or what have you—you also carry emotions with you. With a difficult message, you likely bring stress, anxiety, and perhaps anger and frustration. A typical response to these emotions is defensiveness, which is only human.

How do you diffuse this tension? Start the conversation with four words: "I need your help."

Like defensiveness, it's human nature to want to help people when they ask and when you can. Use our universal human instincts to move the project forward rather than squash it.

Starting with "I need your help" puts both you and the other person in an entirely different emotional place and shifts the energy of the conversation. Rather than being on the offensive and defensive, it brings you together on the same team. Which is truly where you are anyway. Then you can discuss the issue and how to achieve the goal at hand.

Managing conflicts by looking ahead, not behind

Frequently on a team there comes a moment when it becomes clear that two people have an issue. You may not know what it is, but you can see it. An "aha" moment may go something like this: You're in a meeting and team members are sharing info *in* the meeting that really should have been shared *before* the meeting. That means they aren't communicating. However the issue arises, the important thing is to recognize that there are immediate steps and long-range steps that need to be taken.

Get into the right frame of mind

IT'S ABOUT THE PROJECT, NOT THE INDIVIDUALS. Remind yourself and your team of the common goal and the reason you're all there: the end product. Shifting the focus off individuals and toward the shared goal will also shift energy from inward to outward.

DON'T TAKE THINGS PERSONALLY. Business is about people, but it's not personal. You have to think about people and treat people like people, but refrain from taking anything personally.

LET FEELINGS HAPPEN. People get angry and hurt and frustrated. That's okay. Don't internalize it or feel obligated to make them feel better. You have a responsibility to achieve the best end results for the project. Be supportive, but let people feel what they're going to feel, while also making sure the project's moving forward.

STAY NEUTRAL. Whether you're the project manager or a leader, you have to remain neutral and steer clear of any drama. See below for how to fix the drama.

Take action

DON'T CALL ANYONE OUT IN FRONT OF THE GROUP. Don't try and get to the bottom of things in front of the team. This won't help solve the immediate problem.

IN REAL TIME, SUGGEST A SOLUTION. For example, let's say a designer didn't supply a front-end developer with all the rollover graphics for a page. And the designer doesn't like the solution that the developer came up with. Just decide, with the team, what to do: change graphics or keep graphics. Then assign follow-up tasks accordingly.

AFTER THE MEETING, DETERMINE WHAT HAPPENED. Don't bring any assumptions into these conversations or fill in blanks about why things happened as they did. Don't express blame or shame, because pointing fingers won't make anyone feel good, nor will it help the situation. Even if someone dropped the ball, making her feel bad about it won't improve her work, your relationship, or the end product. Once you have the facts, see what you can do to minimize the chance the problem will happen again.

ONE-PERSON CONFLICTS

What happens when the conflict involves only one person? Perhaps someone's creating a bottleneck because they're taking on too much or not delegating enough. Rather than saying, "Why are your projects and tasks getting backed up?" say to her, "Help me help you."

FIND THE ROOT OF THE PROBLEM. The question you ask should *not* be "What went wrong?" The real question is "How can I prevent this problem from happening again?" If you stop your problem solving at "what went wrong," you're missing the point and not truly helping your team work together. You want to figure out the root of the problem—Is the process ineffective? Was there a communication breakdown? Do these two people just not work well together?—*to* ensure it doesn't recur.

MAKE SURE EVERYONE HAS WHAT THEY NEED TO KEEP WORKING. While you address the bigger causes, ask your team, point blank, "Do you have what you need to keep the project moving forward? What else can I do for you?" This might be additional files or a new brief, or it might mean making them feel like they're being heard. Either way, don't let the project sit still while you figure out if anything needs to change on the macro level.

Takeaways

Communication is key to making a project successful. Thinking and analyzing mean nothing if the results of that thinking and analyzing aren't communicated. Emotional intelligence is wasted if you don't adjust your communication to the person or situation. Being the eyes and ears of a project won't be productive if you're not also the mouth.

- Effective communication is open, clear, collaborative, and thorough. Measure your communication against these qualities.

- Being consistent in how and when you communicate will set a calm and responsible tone for your team.

- Take your time when composing and responding to messages and questions; thinking before acting always pays off.

Ultimately, always think about the recipient when you're determining how to communicate; the quality of your communication skills correlates directly with how well she understands.

5

THE PROCESS

Getting digital done right

At Clockwork, our process focuses on the thinking that goes into making an end product effective and the people that make it happen. It's a model that can be used for any interactive product in any environment: It's industry-specific and people-driven.

In this chapter, we'll discuss:

- Existing project management models
- How we manage projects
- The reasoning behind our process

There's more to interactive than foosball and cool offices: It's complicated work and there's a lot at stake.

The remainder of this book takes you through the process we developed at Clockwork. We'll explain the tasks and deliverables that contribute to successful projects. Most importantly, we'll demonstrate how to think critically about delivering interactive work so you can determine how to apply the approach to projects within your environment.

Our process is for us *and* for our clients: It provides shared priorities and collective ownership of the end product. At a strategic level, it gives us something to check against to ensure that we get things right, and helps our clients understand how everything fits together. At a tactical level, our teams choose the tasks and deliverables based on what's appropriate for each project.

Our goal is to change the way people think about how interactive work is defined, developed, and delivered.

Existing project management models

The most well-known and commonly practiced methods of delivering interactive work come from two industries: software development and advertising/marketing.

Most of what's been written about interactive project management is based on two popular software development methods: waterfall and agile. Much of what's practiced is either based on those methods, or is derived from traditional project management processes at advertising agencies (sometimes known as "traffic"). Below are brief overviews of each approach.

WATERFALL. This is a sequential process in which each phase concludes (more or less) before the next phase begins. The project scope is clearly defined early on and phases unfold accordingly. It's a fairly rigid model that allows for little flexibility over the course of the project because a completed phase is more expensive to alter than an in-progress one. Think of a series of locks and dams: once you've progressed through one, you don't turn around and go back through it again. You continue downriver. This model makes a lot of sense for projects that *require* one phase to be completed before starting the next one, like house construction or manufacturing.

AGILE. This model is far less rigid than waterfall—in fact, it's characterized by its lack of formal structure. It incorporates short, cyclical phases into the process to accommodate (and encourage) change. Here, scope is broadly defined at the beginning and the end product gets fleshed out through frequent, iterative releases of the product. Changes and developments occur incrementally, and the direction of the project is continually reassessed. Agile works well in situations where it's acceptable for the definition and scope of a project to evolve over time and where close (even daily) collaboration with clients is possible.

AD AGENCY. This is a generic term we're using to describe a model in which the creative department drives the project vision. Here, the creative team (creative director, art director, and copywriter) has a concept, a big idea, which is then executed across several channels—print, television, radio, and Internet. The creative idea drives the project, and while the clients approve the idea, they are generally not active participants in how that idea is produced.

Versions of these three approaches have been adopted to varying degrees and with varying levels of success by the interactive industry mainly because they were the best available options, and because most interactive teams have emerged from (or within) software or advertising-focused organizations.

Unfortunately, none of these methods work perfectly for client-driven, interactive projects. Waterfall doesn't leave clients enough room for change—and change is inevitable and necessary. Agile projects require a level of deep collaboration that many clients can't commit to, and these projects contain a level of ambiguity with regard to scope that most aren't comfortable with. Lastly, the ad agency model neglects the end user because it emerged from media that is passively consumed, not interacted with. Clients and end-users aside, none of the methods consider the needs of a project team that integrates designers, art directors, and creative directors with programmers, content strategists, and software testers.

Piecing together elements from those models has worked marginally well until now, but the interactive industry is all grown up now; it's time to set aside the hand-me-downs.

It's time to define a process that was designed for us, by us.

YEAH, BUT…What if I don't have any control over how projects are managed?

GLAD YOU ASKED…We know from experience that any interactive team—even one working on a single project inside a non-digital company or agency—can put these ideas to use. You might not be able to decide how projects are managed company-wide, but you can usually decide how your projects are managed. And you never know: Sometimes, a single project's success can influence how other projects are managed.

Clockwork's process

This chapter introduces our process, presented in Figure 5.1. Upcoming chapters will delve into stages within the process. Chapters 6 and 7 explore two aspects of the Research & Planning phase: "Project Prep" and "Project Definition." Chapters 8–10 look at aspects of the Production & Deployment phase: "Project Production," "Project Staging," and "Project Launch." These stages represent distinct moments of convergence between the front-end and back-end tracks—with a deliverable that involves both, like the *development approach* or the *development version*, concluding each stage.

The process we use borrows principles of rigor from waterfall, iterative qualities from agile, and client- and creative-focused techniques from the ad agency models. And it layers in the unique needs of interactive projects and teams. Our combination fits the realities of an interactive project: the range of variables, restrictions, and people.

We initially created this illustration to act as a "you are here" map for project stakeholders. It's useful because it shows who's doing what, and breaks the project into digestible stages. Of course, between each deliverable there are numerous activities, tasks, and meetings. But we concentrated the diagram on the tangible deliverables because they're the elements that affect *every* team member. By using this, everyone knows where they are, what's coming up next, and how deliverables affect subsequent stages.

A clear illustration of the process helps everyone understand and visualize how the project will unfold. Predictability: People love it!

Defining characteristics of our process

ORGANIZED SIMULTANEITY. Multiple people are doing different activities at the same time, and their activities directly affect others. To account for this, we broke the process into two tracks—front-end and back-end—and into two phases. Individuals organize around related tasks, but while working within their own discipline they are also being routinely informed about what's happening among other team members. This organized simultaneity creates a shared and collaborative knowledge base, without creating a wildly inefficient clown car.

GOALS FIRST. Our process has two phases: Research & Planning, and Production & Deployment. During the Research & Planning phase the team determines what to do and why. Once this is firmly established, then the Production & Deployment phase kicks off. At this point, the team confidently and assuredly executes the project.

EFFICIENT AND VERIFIABLE. We are purposeful about what information we capture, and when. Our deliverables are thoughtfully designed to document the critical aspects of the project and leave a trail of thinking and conclusions. They allow the client to see the often-intangible contributions the team makes: the thinking, analyzing, and reasoning. When the deliverables are completed, they're checkpoints; when they're reviewed against, they're guides that keep the project on the right track.

INTENTIONAL SIMPLICITY. Our process contains only what is needed, and no more. We intentionally created *enough* structure: too much creates inefficient busy work; too little and quality suffers. Enough process enhances both quality and efficiency. Importantly, keeping it simple also allows a team of experts the leeway they need to work with a client to set the proper course of a project.

FRONT VS. BACK

By "front-end" we mean everything that the user sees and interacts with, like design and content. By "back-end" we mean the behind-the-scenes code and infrastructure that make the product functional.

"Following a process"—*any* process—shouldn't be confused with "project management." A process is just a guide; project management is thinking and taking action. Remember when we compared the project manager to the conductor of an orchestra? Well, the process is like the sheet music. You need it, but more importantly, you need to inspire a group of talented musicians to play it. Yes, you're going to be inspirational.

Process Overview

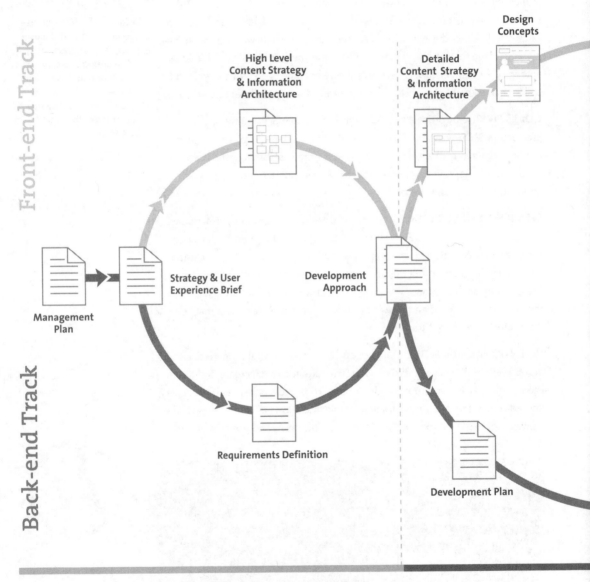

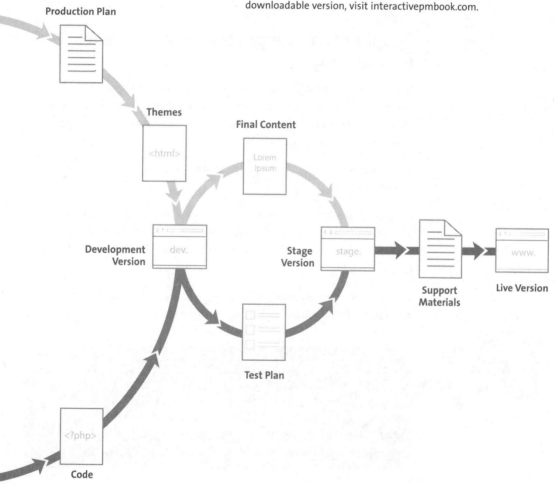

FIGURE 5.1
This view of the process shows the project lifecycle from a deliverables standpoint. This view is helpful because it illustrates the tangible pieces of the process and acts as a "you are here" map. In contrast, a timeline shows the process from a date standpoint. For a downloadable version, visit interactivepmbook.com.

Production Plan

Themes

Final Content

Development Version

Stage Version

Support Materials

Live Version

Test Plan

Code

Production & Deployment

Why it works

These are our beliefs and values about how to manage a project and make a great product. If you're not in a place to adopt our entire process, *read this anyway.*

People drive the process, not the other way around

The process we use at Clockwork reflects team-wide contributions at all points; it not only cultivates collaboration, it requires it. Everyone on the team, throughout the project life cycle, influences the outcome—maintaining this balance requires careful attention.

Balancing everyone's needs and roles is the only way to create a collaborative dynamic.

Developers aren't brought in for only one phase, nor are the designers. Technologists don't drive all the decisions just because these are technology projects, nor can creative professionals or clients simply dictate a "to do" list to the technologists.

Even the way we visualize our process shows this: tasks and phases happen concurrently and there is no hierarchy with regard to the people, deliverables, or tasks.

> The goal of any process is to facilitate getting work done. The process isn't doing its job if it isn't being followed. If teams are going around the process to get something done, look at why. Then ask, do the people need to change their behavior to fit the process, or does the process need to change to fit the people's behavior?

Knowing the *why* makes a difference

Of course teams need to know what to do and by when to do it. But more importantly, they need to know why.

Being a good project manager is about giving context, not just to-dos.

It's the project manager's responsibility to provide a layer of knowledge and service to the team by providing context. Giving orders without context and setting deadlines without working closely with the people doing the work isn't being a leader. It's herding cattle (or cats, depending on where you work). No one wants to be herded and, let's face it, no one wants to herd.

You don't know what clients need, and neither do they (at first)

Scope can't be determined before Research & Planning because neither the client nor the agency truly understands what needs to be built. The findings obtained during planning and research—the scope of the project—are what make a reasonable estimate possible.

Don't propose a solution before you know the problem.

Many times, clients come to agencies with a *solution*: they want a website, or they want an app. But we need to know their *problem*. We can then go about finding a solution to that problem, rather than simply executing what they've asked for. Sometimes they're the same, but other times we come up with an alternative that better suits their short-term and long-term needs or budget.

Surprises are only good at birthday parties

Each stage in our process aims to clarify the project a little more: each document builds on the preceding one to create as complete a picture as possible. As documents are presented to clients, they not only expect them, they also know their *purpose*. The goal is to *continue defining and designing the end product* and *remove any questions about what's being done*.

Clients have a right to know what they're getting.

Of course, part of the reason clients have a right to know what they're getting is because they're paying for something. But the key point is that as a member of the project team, they have expectations and needs, and the internal team has a responsibility to meet them. While they aren't managing the project and dictating exactly how things get done, clients have a right to be up to speed on all the details.

BEYOND THE GANTT

Giving the internal team and the client the full story (the background, the goals, the conversations around the issue) rather than just marching orders will get you farther than any Gantt chart.

ESTIMATE TWICE

We provide two estimates. The first is the cost for doing Research & Planning, during which time we determine scope. Once the scope is defined, we provide an estimate to produce and deploy the project. This second estimate is always presented *after* the Research & Planning phase is completed.

Make a plan, watch it burn

We built accommodations for change into our process. We did this by keeping our overhead low: changes are easy to document, verify, and track. We don't want our internal team members spending four hours updating complicated software whenever a change comes up (sorry, Microsoft Project™, we're looking at you). We want them spending that time on the actual project. They need the right tools, they need to know the end goal, and they need the power to make the right decisions.

The process isn't for the project manager, it's for everybody.

The process is a reference for everyone. It's the way that the final product gets done as well as it can, as efficiently as it can, and as on-target as it can. Perhaps the project manager is the one sending out reminders, or adding documents to the project file, but everyone helps define the process and ensure things are evolving as they should and everyone practices project management at times. Everyone participates. Everyone *gets* to, and everyone *has* to.

When we say we're "process-driven," clients sometimes express hesitation or worry. Perhaps they feel like they won't have control if they follow *our* process. In fact, the opposite is true: it gives them control via knowledge and established expectations and changes are absolutely acceptable (in fact, as you just read, we're counting on it). Our process makes us more flexible, not less so.

Takeaways

The process we follow at Clockwork allows us to:

- Keep our promise of making quality work efficiently.
- Uphold our values of being honest, clear, and collaborative throughout the entire project.

It creates the system through which we do our work and achieve our clients' goals as well as the ones we've set for ourselves.

PROJECT PREP

Put all your ducks in a row

The step *before* planning begins to get everything in order. Once the pitch is accepted, it's tempting to jump into planning and research. But taking extra time to align team members pays off. Plus, it sets everything and everybody up so the planning stage is effective.

In this chapter, we'll discuss

- Why prep is necessary
- Getting started: Creating a team and initiating a project
- Kicking it off: Connecting with the client
- Preparing the management plan: Gathering details

IN THIS
CHAPTER

This is when the project manager drafts the plan for how the project will get done, from who's working on it to what's being assumed to what risks are lurking under the metaphorical bed.

The prep is the "pre-" part of the project. It's when and how everyone gets on the same page so that the "during" part is done well.

Be prepared

The prep stage grew out of our recognition that defining how the project will be managed—on both the client and internal sides—needed to be an official part of the process, not just a throwaway assumption. Moving from the brainstorming and creative ideas that sell a project to a concrete definition of what will be delivered is hard. Prep starts that transition.

Thinking through—and documenting—*how* everything is going to get done is as important as *getting* it done. Determining roles and responsibilities is a key step in making sure that the team starts from a shared understanding.

Start on the right foot

VOCAB REMINDER!

When we say *product*, we mean whatever digital deliverable your team is building for the client. For example, it could be a mobile app, a website, or a web application.

Once the client agrees to the project, the prep stage begins.

Choose team members

Here's where you begin to think about how the work is *really* all going to get done. Who's needed? Who's not? What team would be best for this client and this end product? To figure it out, it's best to think about two aspects of the project: the deliverables and the personality of the project.

Assess deliverables

Think about what you know, think about your current needs, and consider what you'll probably need in the future. At this point, bring on the people who must be involved.

We start by assigning the four roles that play the biggest part in research and planning: strategist, tech lead, creative lead, and tester.

For the other project roles, we often wait until after the development approach (discussed in Chapter 7). Until you know the exact project scope, you may not be able to choose the full, final team.

> *YEAH, BUT…How do I know who must be involved?*
>
> *GLAD YOU ASKED…If the project includes both front- and back-end development, all four roles are almost always needed right up front. But if you're only delivering creative perhaps you wouldn't need a tech lead. Conversely, if your developers are building someone else's design, perhaps you wouldn't need a creative lead.*

Match personalities

There are also more nuanced elements to think about when putting together a team. Think through the personalities of both the project *and* the people. Certain details in the proposal or about the client can help you get a feel for what the project will be like: Is the client a big corporation or an independent business? Is the deliverable well defined? Is the end product a boundary-pushing endeavor or a straightforward classic?

Taking all this into account, determine which soft skills fit with a project. Different people work best under different conditions. To the best of your ability, match people's personalities with the project's personality. For example, if you've got a person on the team who works best on very structured projects, she might not work well on the cutting-edge, high-stress project with the startup client. In the end, whether you get your dream team or not, at least you'll have thought through details that will make your team perform its best.

While we never have a B-team, we still have to assemble the right A-team.

WHAT IS A STRATEGIST?

The strategist is the person constantly assessing projects with the goals and strategies in mind. The role of strategist varies from agency to agency; at many traditional agencies the account person performs this role. See Figure 1.1 for a refresher on roles.

ASK AROUND

If you can't get your head around the project personality with the information you know, ask the sales or account team member who worked with the client in the pitch or proposal phase. At this point, she will have talked to the client more than anyone else on the internal team.

THINK ABOUT: Requesting a team

Getting to handpick your entire team is rare. Here's our advice: Always request the people you'd like and explain why you want them on the project. Maybe someone's worked with the client before on another project and it went really, really well. Even if your ideal person appears to be unable to work on your project, you don't know until you ask. And there's that old adage about a squeaky wheel. So, go ahead and squeak.

Sometimes there will be people on your team who don't want to work on the project. In ad agencies, print designers may fill in on interactive projects. (It shouldn't happen, but it does.) Use some of the tips from Chapter 3, "Emotional Intelligence," to get through any rough patches. Acknowledge the situation ("I understand that this isn't your favorite kind of work") and see if there's anything you can do to help make it more manageable for her ("Help me help you").

Hold an initiation meeting

The initiation meeting is for internal team members only. It's a chance for the client-facing team members to fill in the rest of the team on the information and discussions that have transpired with the client.

BRING IN A TESTER NOW?

It might seem early to invite a tester to the initiation meeting, but the cost of having your tester at the table for this meeting pays for itself in the value she brings in understanding the project from start to finish.

It's tempting to look at a proposal (or estimate or scope of work) as the whole story. But there's always a boatload of information gleaned from conversations and interactions that never makes it into writing. And maybe it shouldn't (it's interpretations, feelings, perceptions, and politics), but it *should* be shared and discussed.

At a minimum, the strategist, creative lead, tech lead, and tester should attend the meeting.

Find out what we know about the client

Think of this meeting as a massive brain dump in which everything that's known about the project and the client is shared with the team. They get the lowdown from whoever has interacted with the client up until now—frequently it's the sales, business development, or account management teams.

Knowing what's happened between your team and the client helps you figure out the client's personality, which in turn shapes the personality of the project. Knowing the personality of the project helps to determine the appropriate management style and the format of deliverables. Is it a technology-heavy project that requires months of iterations (therefore, repetitive and focused)? Is the client determined to have a cutting-edge product (that is, cool and creative)? Is the client ultrasensitive to aesthetics (that is, prizes design over technology)?

These client-side details help the project manager, and the team, think about the best ways to move the project forward smoothly.

Find out what the client knows about us

The initiation meeting is also the time when the client-facing team communicates what's been promised to the client and what sold them on working with your company.

The best way to do this is review the pitch or proposal. Let everyone see what the client saw, what promises were made ("We can definitely have a site done in three months."), and what ballparks were given ("We usually turn projects of this scope around in three months.").

This level of information provides the internal team with a snapshot of what the client knows. That kind of detail allows your team to better see things from the client's perspective and cuts down on assumptions ("Wait, who told the client it was going to be three months?!").

WHAT'S NOT BEING SAID?

At this stage, there are many things about the client and project that you won't know. Ask your team as many questions as you can to get as much information as you can. Errors of omission are the hardest errors to catch; questions help prevent these.

> Your process should be a manifestation of your values. The front-line team needs to be honest about what's possible and how it can or can't happen. If the company values communicated in the pitch and those being actualized in your work align, the transition from sales to project implementation will be that much easier.

YEAH BUT...What if there's a discrepancy between the team members talking about the work and the team members doing the work?

GLAD YOU ASKED...The team is in a challenging position if your client-facing team members don't join meetings, if they don't share information, or if they make promises the rest of the team can't keep. If it happens, address this within your project team: Start by acknowledging the gap, identify the discrepancy between the promises and the reality, and follow up by brainstorming solutions that will better align the outward and inward realities.

Connect with the client

Now that you've done the internal prep work, it's time to get in front of the client.

Hold a kickoff meeting

This is the first (and sometimes the only) opportunity for the client to tell their story to the entire internal team. By having everyone in the room together—both internally and client side—we ensure a chance for every person to connect with the client at least once. And this is the perfect opportunity to cultivate a celebratory shared experience across the team.

USE THE MANAGEMENT PLAN

Start a draft of the management plan (discussed below) to use as an agenda and workbook for the meeting. It includes the key issues that need to be talked about— stakeholders, initial goals, etc. Highlight all the blanks and use them as guides to get the information you need.

This is all great, because having these exciting moments with one another creates a bond that will translate into collaborative energy later on. The kickoff meeting achieves both practical and emotional goals, both of which are important. It's amazing how far face-to-face contact goes in establishing a productive, collaborative working relationship.

Making the kickoff meeting successful

On a practical level, you're accomplishing three things here: getting as many project details as you can, demonstrating to the client that you're prepared and enthusiastic about the project, and transitioning the client from the sales team to the project team.

FRAME QUESTIONS APPROPRIATELY. For example, if you read in the proposal that the project stemmed from a previous product, frame your question accordingly: "We read about the history of this project in the proposal. Can you tell us more about that? We'd like to hear it directly from you." This will communicate to them that you did your homework, while allowing you to dig deeper in person.

KEEP THE ENERGY POSITIVE. While the team is gathering information and listening to stories that inform the project, be sure that you're all showing active interest. The client is probably feeling a lot of things at this stage; they're about to embark on something big and exciting, but also potentially stressful. Your internal team can have a reassuring effect on the client by displaying positivity.

TIP: Don't force the agenda

Details and project minutiae can be deflating in the face of a client who wants to talk big ideas or grand goals. While details *do* need to be worked out at some point, that can always be done later, if necessary. As the project manager, figure out who the main client contact is. If nothing else, you can follow up with that person after the meeting to start hashing out the day-to-day details. This shows that you're on top of the pragmatic stuff, but it won't detract from the eyes-on-the-prize energy.

HAVE A TRANSITION PLAN. Over the duration of the meeting, it's critical to pass the baton from the pitch team to the full project team. The team members with an existing relationship with the client should start off the meeting. As the meeting progresses, the new project team should play more and more of a role in the conversation. By the end, you want the client to feel good about the project manager being their new primary contact.

ENCOURAGE CONNECTION. On an emotional level, the kickoff meeting is a chance for everyone to have a shared experience. The kickoff makes everyone feel like they're on the same team; there are faces to place with names, and real-life moments to complement emails. Moreover, the meeting provides a chance for the internal team to feel the client's energy firsthand. This generates care and concern, and conquering challenges is much easier when you care.

TALK PROCESS. Wrap up the kickoff meeting by walking through your process. We explain all the phases and expectations so nothing's a surprise. We emphasize our values and how they translate into the process itself. If possible, we outline tactical details that will help us determine how we'll manage the project, like if the client has preferences or expectations with regard to meeting types and frequency, and who should be included in status emails.

PRACTICE THE HANDOFF

Don't assume a handoff will happen organically because it isn't an easy thing to do well. And if it's done poorly, the client may feel like they're being passed off. Rehearse how to direct the conversation so it goes smoothly.

Successful meetings don't just happen

The kickoff meeting is one of the few times where it's totally fine to put together an agenda, and then not follow it. The goal of this meeting is to establish a connection and a relationship.

Management Plan
aka The Rules of Engagement

The management plan outlines the rules of engagement for the team. It centralizes information and articulates how the project will be managed.

OWNER:

PROJECT MANAGER

CONTRIBUTORS:

ACCOUNT STRATEGIST   CREATIVE LEAD   CLIENT   PRODUCTION LEAD   TECH LEAD

RELATIONSHIP MANAGER   TESTER   USER EXPERIENCE ARCHITECT

DESCRIPTION:

This document is the road map for a successful project. It provides the team with two primary types of information: logistical details and big picture facts that affect the overall project.

The logistical details found in the communication plan and contact list establish collective understanding of who's doing what and how the project will unfold. The project-wide risks, assumptions, and dependencies are captured here in clearly defined terms. These can be the difference between success and failure because they call out information that has the potential to derail a project.

This document shapes the way people and individual project components will be managed.

SPECIAL CONSIDERATIONS:

• As the first project document, use it to set the tone for all reviewing and collaborating and approving as you go forward.

• Embrace risks! Challenge your team and client to think of as many risks and assumptions as possible; there are plenty.

• Revise and update this document. Don't set it and forget it!

LOCATION IN THE PROCESS:

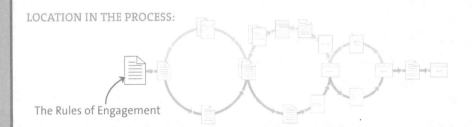

The Rules of Engagement

This meeting in particular requires a lot of emotional intelligence to be managed well: If it skews too emotional ("Hey! Yay! We're all excited! Fun!") it risks being a waste of a lot of people's (billable) time. If it skews too practical ("And now I'd like to draw your attention to the second paragraph on page 14 where we outline risk 17…") it risks being a buzzkill, which is no way to get a successful client relationship off the ground.

So, while there should be some structure and preparation for the meeting (that's what an agenda provides), the energy in the moment should determine how it unfolds.

Prepare the management plan

All the questions and answers you gather here feed into the primary prep document, the *management plan* (Cheat Sheet 001). This section contains the thinking and planning that go into making the management plan accurate and effective.

Outline project

At this point in the project, you likely know only preliminary details about the project. The key pieces of information you want to start compiling are: assumptions, deliverables, and dependencies.

List assumptions

Assumptions feel so obvious that you may not even think they need to be stated. That's why they're so insidious. But sitting down with your internal team and reviewing the project to clarify exactly what's being assumed—and confirming these assumptions with the client—prevents bumps in the road later.

Unspoken assumptions can create chasms of misunderstanding between your company and the client. And calling them out early illuminates many behind-the-scenes details that can be overlooked.

Here are a few examples of assumptions:

- Clockwork will provide content strategy and page buildout; client will be responsible for writing copy.

- Client will provide brand guidelines and brand assets.

- Clockwork will source stock photography for the project and provide a separate estimate for photo pricing.

- Product data will be provided in a single CSV file.

Start training your internal team and the client to think about assumptions as they go about their work. Capture any that you agree upon in the management plan, and as things progress update the list to accurately reflect the project.

Define deliverables

Our deliverables list doesn't just include the end product; it also lists the deliverables that are created in service of the end product.

As with all projects, there are many layers of work that contribute to digital products. There might be stakeholder interviews, design concepts, and high-level wireframes. All of these are *things* that get delivered and are owned by the client. We articulate each and every one of these *and* the format in which they'll be handed over, such as JPG, PSD, or code. This ensures that clients understand what tangible artifacts they'll be receiving (or seeing) along the way.

Determine dependencies

Dependencies are conditions that dictate things that *must* or *can't* happen for the project to get done; they are details that constrain the project and have the potential to jeopardize it.

There are three common scenarios in which dependencies arise: when your team is using third-party products, when you build something that's being integrated into another system, and when legal approval is needed. In the first two cases, the end product is dependent on that third party or system to operate correctly. Legal approval isn't *always* a dependency, but it's a classic project derailer. Determine at the beginning of the project if the release or launch hinges on a legal team approving the small print and how much time they need to review.

There will be other dependencies. Think carefully and critically about what they might be, and write them down.

Develop a communication plan

Establish when, how, and with whom communication happens. Giving a preview of what communication will look like throughout the project increases the likelihood that communication will be effective. And if you don't set expectations, the client will set them for you. Then you'll find yourself reacting to their style—which could be anything from catch-me-if-you-can to shotgun emails.

Plan scheduled communication

Determine email aliases and set time and day details for status meeting and status reports.

Think about these details now because it may require a few conversations with the client before nailing down the exact stakeholders and determining the most effective schedule.

Ultimately, all this information is clearly listed in the management plan so there's a single reference that illustrates what people should expect and when.

Articulate a review process

Outline the review and approval process as clearly as possible so that everyone knows how work will be routed and when and by whom it is approved.

At Clockwork, we begin every project with the following four-step review process that starts the conversation. The key detail to define is how many rounds of revisions qualify as "in scope."

- Internal review

- Full team review—round 1

- Gather feedback and determine changes

- Full team review—round 2, with a date by which feedback must be received

Does anything ever happen in four steps like this? Of course not—but you have to start somewhere! Figuring out these details seems like a no-brainer, but going that next step and writing them down in a shared document makes a huge difference.

NAMING CONVENTIONS

Tiny details make such a difference! Give the project a "shortname" to be used in every project filename and directory. This makes organization easy and consistent.

USE YOUR DELIVERABLES LIST

Refer to your list of deliverables and ask your client who will approve each document. This will help them think of things like, "Oh, the copy deck? I'm going to need to get signoff from both legal and marketing on that." Remembering that now is fantastic. Remembering it a week before launch can be fatal.

Encourage the client to have one person on their end wrangle feedback and approvals. That person doesn't have to be the *approver* of each deliverable, but she is responsible for gathering and then communicating that approval to the team.

Determine approval requirements

Determine if there are final approvers: the people on the client side who have the final yes/no vote. Approvers may fluctuate depending on the deliverable or phase—designs may go through a creative director whereas feature lists or information architecture might go through the marketing director. But nailing down who approves what ensures that there are no surprises later.

Timelines for executive and legal approvals are often mismeasured or overlooked entirely. For both groups, timing is key. Often legal departments have turnaround times of two weeks or more, and executive schedules can be extremely busy. Waiting until the very end to show deliverables to higher-ups can be detrimental, while showing them too early can be premature.

Finding a balance of how and when deliverables are routed is up to the client, but it's critical to get everyone thinking about it early on.

TIP: Keep the team as small as possible

It may be hard to get the client to limit the group of approvers to just a few people. Stick to your guns. Any project that's decided by committee is compromised. It's impossible to effectively manage scope, timeline, and budget while being bombarded with correspondence and feedback from numerous people. Frame it up like, "I need your help managing feedback to ensure we hit our deadline." That's a statement most clients appreciate hearing.

Assess project risks

Assessing risks measures the project against harsh realities.

If you *think* something might go wrong, it probably will. Risk assessment means forecasting problems that are likely to crop up, creating a plan to avoid them, and thinking about how to address them if they do occur. Like assumptions, there will be many and it's better to call out as many as possible in the beginning.

As a starting point, we have a list of standard risks that we plan for in almost every project. We always include this list, first, because they're the head-slappers. They're risks that apply to just about any project. Second, having a standard list to start from means that team members can direct their energy toward the *project-specific* risks. Common factors to consider when determining additional risks are: security, infrastructure, process, communication, software, third-party vendors, dependencies on another project or team, client expectations, and fraud.

The purpose of isolating risks is to develop plans for managing them. We want to proactively minimize the risks, not just know what they are. So, in addition to the risks themselves, it is imperative that you think about what can be done to mitigate those risks.

Here are our standard risks with their corresponding mitigation plans:

DELAYED DELIVERY OF ASSETS. The project manager will stay in touch with the client to flag any upcoming delays early on and adjust the project timeline as necessary.

DELAYED CLIENT FEEDBACK. The project timeline will establish expectations for feedback at the project outset. The project manager will flag any delays early on and adjust the project timeline as necessary.

INCOMPLETE OR INACCURATE REQUIREMENTS. Clockwork writes—and routes for approval—a requirements definition (RD) document. Project work commences when the RD is approved by both parties. Clockwork will create a change order document if additional requirements are identified after the approval of the initial RD.

TIP: Explain the purpose of risks to client

Seeing all those risks on paper can really freak a client out—especially this early in the project. ("You're telling me we might fail and we haven't even started yet?") Be sure to explain the purpose of the risk assessment; you're not saying that they *will* happen, simply that they *could*. You're listing them so the team can be vigilant in spotting them early and, most importantly, you're thinking about how to actively avoid them.

SCOPE CREEP. The Clockwork project manager will notify the client if decisions are affecting scope and deliver change orders for approval as necessary.

ASK AROUND

Ask your team and your client if they can think of any red flags from their vantage point. A great way to phrase your question is "what if...?" If they respond, "Oh, that'll never happen," it may not be a risk for the project. If the response is a furrowed brow, you probably have a risk on your hands.

You can't prevent every risk, but by putting them in writing, you're putting the whole team on alert. Each team member is a watchdog who sees different dimensions of the project. Having everyone on the lookout for all the possible risks while they're knee-deep in their part of the project is just smart.

Write mitigation plans with care

It's important to give project-specific contexts and a solution-focused mitigation plan when presenting risks to the team so they don't feel like you're calling them out. Sometimes risks can make team members defensive because they bring attention to a possible weak spot. Providing context and explanation when raising risks will minimize the likelihood of two possible consequences:

- Making it sound like you're anticipating people not doing their jobs.

- Making it sound like you're preparing for failure.

Takeaways

The prep part of the project is a great time to get high-level issues outlined. It's when the project manager and the whole team figure out how the project will play out, take life, and become a real end product.

Meetings and conversations are the primary deliverables as the team outlines details and brainstorms project information. In the end, the management plan captures these facts and establishes communication plans and other housekeeping details.

7

PROJECT DEFINITION

Assess, outline, align

If you were building a house, would you start nailing two-by-fours together without a blueprint? Let's hope not.

Aligning the project goals with the realities of the current landscape is how effective solutions are defined. *Then* we can start nailing two-by-fours together.

In this chapter, we'll discuss

- Defining why: Gathering information and insights

- Creating a plan: Determining what's needed

- Convergence: Recommending a solution

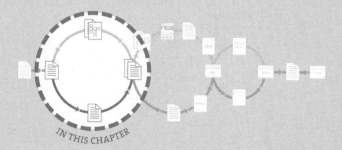

IN THIS CHAPTER

I t's important to clearly outline goals before designing a screen or writing a line of code. This is what's achieved in this stage of the Research & Planning phase.

In this phase, you're gathering the necessary information to understand the client's needs and determine the right solutions for them and the end user. As we mentioned in Chapter 5, clients sometimes come to the table with a particular solution in mind. Through the tasks completed in the Research & Planning phase, you verify their suggestion or recommend another route.

The right solution may not be the coolest idea or the newest technology; sometimes it's simply the best possible option given the audience, timing, and budget. At the end of this phase, the *right* solution will be defined.

Successful interactive projects meet the client's goals and the end user's needs within the parameters of time and budget.

Project management checkpoint

The strategist and project manager divide and conquer during the project definition stage. Their shared goal is to determine the best end product, but they're focusing on different things. The strategist guides the thinking while the project manager guides the doing.

FACT: Documents aren't the only deliverables

Clients and teams can get caught up in documents because they're tangible.

Keep in mind that the *real* deliverables are thinking, analyzing, planning, and deciding. Documents simply capture those activities; they don't replace them.

Strategy and User Experience Brief

aka The North Star

This document keeps the project and team on the right path and remains the constant marker of where the project is going.

OWNER:

ACCOUNT STRATEGIST

CONTRIBUTORS:

PROJECT MANAGER | USER EXPERIENCE ARCHITECT | CREATIVE LEAD | PRODUCTION LEAD | TECH LEAD

RELATIONSHIP MANAGER | CONTENT STRATEGIST

DESCRIPTION:

The brief contains three primary elements: an assessment of the current landscape, where the client wants to be, and what needs to happen in order to get there.

The brief is a summary of a lot of research activities. The current landscape and where the client wants to be are determined though interviews, assessments, evaluations, and reviews. With the information that's captured, the team isolates the client's goals.

The strategy and user experience brief is the plan to achieve the specified goals.

SPECIAL CONSIDERATIONS:

• This document requires a lot of collaboration. It takes a village!

• Get this document just right or your project will start off on the wrong foot. The compass needs to be spot-on to work.

• Contributors will vary depending on project scope.

LOCATION IN THE PROCESS:

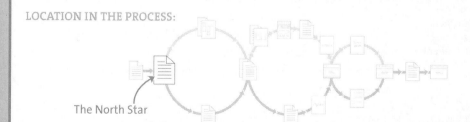

The North Star

Define the goals and how to reach them

DON'T SKIP THE BRIEF

If you already use a creative brief, don't just skip the strategy and UX brief. Make sure the points outlined below are included in it, or create a complementary document (or addendum) for interactive projects.

After the kickoff meeting, the strategist starts putting together what we call the strategy and user experience (UX) brief (Cheat Sheet 002). Call it whatever you like—or even roll it into an existing document in your process—but what's important is to create a document that guides all subsequent elements of a project: content, user experience architecture, design, development, and quality assurance.

The team's strategic thinking is captured through a series of exercises, and is then compiled into the full report. The brief provides information about any existing brand standards or creative direction, defines the target audiences, and becomes the litmus test for the end product.

Strategy means different things to different people. And frequently it's used without a lot of specificity. For this reason, we're very clear about what we're delivering when we use the term: a comprehensive plan to achieve specific goals for digital initiatives.

Assess the current landscape

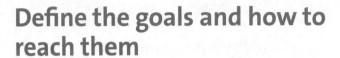

SPEND WISELY

Only do exercises that you need to do. Each task costs time and money; spend the client's money like it's your own. Use any existing client work or data to help complete the picture of the current landscape.

Assessing the current landscape means determining where the client and the product are *today*. Once that is well understood, the team can provide better direction about where to go and how to get there.

But, "current landscape" could mean a lot of things. To prevent the team from getting bogged down in an approach that's too broad, the strategist should focus on what *must* be known to move forward while the project manager considers how much time and money is available during this stage. Each assessment exercise provides valuable information, but which information is most valuable depends on the project. Determine the highest-value information, and begin there.

What you need to find out

As the brief is created, ask the following questions. The answers help determine which exercises to do and what information to present to the client.

- What do we need to know about the client and users to make the most suitable end product for their needs?

- What information will help determine objectives and desires that may not be obvious?

- How does the available technology or software influence or impact the solution?

- What current problems in the client's industry, business, or process could be helped by the end product?

- How much time is available to complete these assessments? What is the budget?

Project management checkpoint

To put together an effective assessment plan, the project manager must understand resources and the strategist must understand the requirements and scope of each exercise. They decide which team member should do each task and what exercises should be done.

Then they work together to move forward economically, efficiently, and successfully. Ultimately, many people contribute. The challenge is getting everything done without people stepping all over one another.

Complete assessment exercises

Each assessment exercise will result in a collection of data that's shared with the client at the end of Research & Planning (it is, after all, their data). But, the data on its own isn't the important part; the critical deliverable is the *meaning* of the data, outlined in the strategy and UX brief.

COMPETITIVE REVIEWS. These are reviews of similar products or companies with similar brand messaging. At times, clients will come prepared with reviews. If they do, use them!

You will learn how similar messages and products are communicated, design standards within the client's industry, and effectiveness of related features and functionality.

CONTENT AUDIT. This is a review of the content (copy, imagery, videos, audio) and its organization in an existing product, or content created for a new product.

You will learn the amount and types of content, how content fits with new goals and strategies, and what content needs to be edited or added.

FUNCTIONALITY AUDIT. This is a description of how the current product functions on the user side, and how it interacts with internal client systems. A usability lab may also be conducted to see how users react and respond to functionality (more on that later in this chapter).

You will learn how existing elements work, how features interact with each other, whether the site architecture and functionality work well together, and how well features support or manage business processes.

TECHNOLOGY AUDIT. This assesses the technology currently being used, including things like content management systems, development languages, and software platforms.

You will learn what legacy systems and databases are being used and how they interact, how data is entered and stored, and which third-party services, sites, and applications are used.

THE DATA DEFENSE

Keep the data handy, and use it to support your recommendations whenever possible. If ideas are backed up by data, it's easy for the client to see the logic and approve the suggestion.

DATA ANALYSIS. Ask your client for as much data as they can give you. Web analytics are an easy first step, but they're just a snapshot of trends and patterns. There's often more data at other sources. For example, if they have an e-commerce website, their database will give the real story of their completed orders. If it's an app sold through iTunes, there are app sales and crash reports available.

The strategist should consult with the whole team about what data would be helpful; the project manager should work with the client to request it. The team member who analyzes the data depends on what is received; something like crash reports will likely be analyzed by a tech lead, while web stats may be reviewed by the strategist or a business analyst.

INTERVIEWS. Interviews produce qualitative data based on discussion in a one-on-one or group setting. You get highly personalized answers that are direct responses to real-time questions. The live nature of the interview means that follow-up questions can be adjusted based on answers. The challenge is that data is entirely unique, making it time consuming to compile and review.

USERS. Conduct interviews with current product users to determine how they use it and what could be changed.

You will learn how users interact with and feel about the product, and their perspective on both messaging and functionality.

STAKEHOLDERS. Conduct interviews with current stakeholders to gather their ideas and assessments about the product.

You will learn what they need the product to do, organizational challenges that will affect how the project unfolds on the client side, how they understand project goals, and any ideas they have for design and functionality.

SURVEYS. Surveys are a relatively inexpensive way to obtain quantitative data about a product quickly. They can be conducted electronically (email or website prompt), over the phone, or in person. Preformatted answers make the data easier to compile and analyze.

USERS. Survey current users to determine how they use an existing product.

You will learn demographics, how they interact with and feel about the product, and their opinions about messaging and functionality.

STAKEHOLDERS. Survey current stakeholders to determine how they use the product.

You will learn how they use the product, how well the existing product meets their needs, how they understand project messaging and goals, and any ideas they have for design or functionality.

USABILITY LAB (U-LAB). Hands-on, real-time interaction with the product is a great way to review what the user is actually doing when using the product. U-labs can range from do-it-yourself setups to fancy rental facilities with two-way mirrors. The key to success with either approach is how well the sessions are facilitated.

The strategist will help determine the questions and scenarios, but other team members, or an outside facilitator, may administer them. Clients may want to observe the sessions live (via an observation room or a livestream) or review recorded footage later.

You will learn how users talk about the product, whether the product meets their needs, and differences between *expected* and *actual* user interaction.

PRESENTING ASSESSMENTS

You may end up generating a lot of information during this stage. This is valuable for the client, and for the project, so do what you can to illustrate data, provide overviews and excerpts, call out key findings, and provide interpretations and recommendations. There's a story in your data; find the best way to tell it.

Determine where the project is going

Use findings from the assessment exercise to identify where the project needs to go. With the problems, challenges, and visions in mind, articulate what the end product needs to achieve, and some ways to achieve it.

Set goals, strategies, and tactics

The distinctions between goals, strategies, and tactics are *very* important. We go to great lengths to articulate this to our teams because writing them accurately in the strategy and UX brief steers the project in the right direction.[2]

GOALS. These are big, sweeping things that serve the primary function of the organization. They're why you're doing what you're doing. They should be neither too broad nor too specific. When thinking through how a product is going

---

1 New Riders, 2010

2 This section is adapted from a blog post by our colleague, Michael Koppelman, http://www.clockwork.net/blog/2010/02/11/382/goals_strategies_and_tactics.

to work, the goals are like a bouncer: they determine what's in and what's out. If an element of the project isn't serving at least one goal, it's not necessary.

STRATEGIES. These are conceptual, nonspecific ways to achieve the goals. They are *what* you're doing. Strategies are broad plans to achieve the stated goals. They're actions, but ones that could be executed in a number of ways.

TACTICS. Tactics are experiments. They're *how* you're going to execute the strategies that will achieve the goals. They're the most nimble part of the overall strategy: if they aren't moving the product toward the goals, new tactics are implemented.

There will be some back and forth with the client to fine-tune goals and strategies. That's perfect. Stating them clearly, concisely, and accurately sets up the project and the team for success. These goals will be referenced throughout the project, so it's best to get them to a point where everyone has the "Yes, that's it!" moment. Then they're done.

Project management checkpoint

As with the assessment exercises, the strategist and project manager are wrangling people and ideas as the goals are being finalized. Thinking and planning are critical to isolating and defining project goals.

It requires a combination of analyzing what's in front of you, and translating information or ideas into actionable goals. With your client and team, you're determining where the project can—and should—go. Keep the team focused on goals and strategies so the direction remains clear and precise.

FUZZY METRICS ARE OKAY

Sometimes goals will not have quantifiable metrics. Take this goal as an example: "We want our employees to feel good about using the new website." That's a valid goal, but it has to be measured qualitatively, not quantitatively. As an example, we might suggest, "The client will obtain anecdotal accounts from employees to assess their experience."

Move from brief to plan

Next up? The team determines how to turn the strategy and UX brief into a plan for a real product.

The documents—high-level information architecture and content strategy and the requirements definition—build on what was provided in the brief and begin to form a project plan. Here, tactics start taking clearer shape.

Create a method amid the madness

From here on out, everything is happening more or less at the same time, but we'll talk about them in a linear fashion because it's a book, and that's how books work. The simplest way to start to make sense of this is to divide the work into what the user sees and interacts with (the front-end track) and what's "under the hood" (the back-end track).

It isn't this clear-cut in real life—of course, the designers and developers are often working together—but each track has different considerations and deliverables. That's what the project manager is for: to figure out the best way to achieve what needs to be done in a way that makes sense for the immediate project.

Coordinate people

At this point, it's critical to find a balance between working together as a team, and working separately in respective expertise areas.

While the deliverables are distinct, they are also complementary. The information architecture can't represent an interaction that isn't possible from a development standpoint, and the requirements definition can't contain a feature for which the user experience hasn't been considered. Ultimately, the internal team needs to reach consensus and this requires the project manager's full attention.

How teams work together in this stage varies, but it should be a healthy tug-of-war among the following members:

CLIENT: "Here's what we want…"

USER EXPERIENCE ARCHITECT: "Here's what's going to be best for the users…"

CONTENT STRATEGIST: "Here are the messages and information we have to communicate…"

DEVELOPERS: "Here's the functionality that will create a successful product…"

PROJECT MANAGER: "Hey guys, this is due on Friday and we're trending a little over on budget…"

And this is all happening simultaneously. As Figure 7.1 shows, there are several layers to *every* interactive product. The project manager determines how it unfolds with a collaborative dynamic.

Concrete   Completion

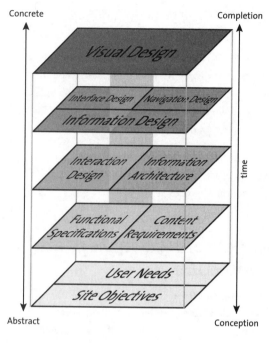

Abstract   Conception

http://www.jjg.net/ia/

FIGURE 7.1
This graphic shows the layers of considerations for developing a thoughtful user experience. Each discipline has to work closely with the others to account for the constraints and produce the best solution possible.

How to coordinate

ARBITRATE CONVERSATIONS. Every team member will make recommendations within his area of expertise. That's necessary to arrive at the right solutions. But it might take some tough conversations between expertise areas to get there. At this point, the project manager should moderate these conversations and determine how the problems are going to be solved *together*.

NEUTRALLY ASSESS OPTIONS. When expertise areas have conflicting ideas, it's necessary for a third party (cue: project manager) to step in and be a neutral, goal-focused opinion.

CREATE A PRODUCTIVE ENVIRONMENT. It takes working both together and independently to reach good decisions and create excellent deliverables, and there are pros and cons to each approach.

WORKING SESSIONS. This is the most actively collaborative way to work together. Everyone gets in a room and hashes things out. The pro is that the left hand knows what the right hand is doing. The con? It can be expensive to have the team all working together, and completing work by committee can be ineffective.

CREATING DOCUMENTS SEPARATELY. At times, having the expertise areas go off on their own to create their respective documents and share them with the team as a whole to get feedback is the way to go. On the up side, work gets done quickly. The down side is that groups can end up going in two different directions if they're not in contact with one another.

Think about what's best for the project and the team to find a balance between these modes of working. Each project will have a different point where quality and efficiency are equalized.

Complete high-level content strategy and information architecture

ROLE ASSIGNMENT

For small projects, content and UXA might be just one person, while for larger projects it will be multiple people. What's important is that the right questions are being asked, and answered.

The first step for the content strategy and user experience architecture (UXA) teams is to determine the exact deliverables needed to outline a plan. At this stage, it's important to remember that this is *high-level* stuff; it isn't detailed or fully hashed out (Cheat Sheet 003).

Content strategy

The content team determines how to deliver key messages and the types of content that support project objectives. They isolate objectives for individual pages and screens, and assess what content will support those objectives. They determine what content will make interactions logical and easy.

LEARN MORE: Recommended reading

We're just skimming the surface here. And some smart people have written books about both content strategy and information architecture. Check out *Content Strategy for the Web* by Kristina Halvorson[3] and *Don't Make Me Think: A Common Sense Approach to Web Usability* by Steve Krug.[4]

---

3 New Riders, 2009

4 Que Publishing, 2000

High-level Content Strategy & Information Architecture aka The Framework

High level content strategy and information architecture (IA) provide schematics that structure the design and development of the product.

OWNERS:

USER EXPERIENCE
ARCHITECT

CONTENT STRATEGIST

CONTRIBUTORS:

CREATIVE LEAD

DESIGNER

ACCOUNT
STRATEGIST

CLIENT

DESCRIPTION:

High-level content strategy is the assessing of and planning for content that meets project goals and intended messaging. High-level IA translates business objectives and user goals into diagrams and schematics that recommend an overall structure to the end product.

Commonly, content inventories and audits are started at this point to assess how much content will be needed and to establish a messaging strategy. IA begins with stakeholder interviews, user interviews, and surveys, and is delivered in a set of documents including sitemaps and wireframes.

Deliverables for high-level content strategy and IA fluctuate with each project. At this stage, the goal is to understand how much work needs to be done to build the recommended digital solution.

SPECIAL CONSIDERATIONS:

- Complete all IA in parallel with developers as they create the requirements definition.

- All team members must reference these deliverables often throughout the evolution of your project.

- Make sure design and functionality align with IA and content strategy.

LOCATION IN THE PROCESS:

The Framework

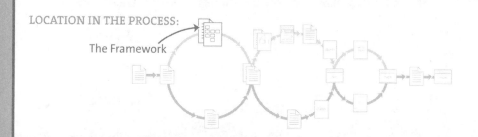

Commonly, the content strategist is completing two tasks at this high-level stage: performing a content audit and collaborating with the user experience architect and tech lead to ensure that high-level information architecture and requirements definition support the identified content needs.

While the client may get more excited about particular features or designs, content is truly the bedrock of every product. Consider content early and from all angles to create products that effective connect with users—which is the ultimate victory for every project.

High-level information architecture

At this stage, information architecture (IA) deliverables propose how information will be organized and how the user will interact with features and content. The purpose of doing the high-level exercises is to better understand project scope (Are there 5 screens in the app, or 50?) and get an idea of the amount of work it will take to create the end product. The most common deliverables are described below and examples are shown in Figure 7.2.

SITE MAP. These show the organization and structure of a website or app through simple illustrations. They illustrate the relationship between pages, sections, and navigation.

USER FLOW DIAGRAMS. These diagrams chart the paths that a user might take to navigate the product. These help clients understand how users might progress through a series of steps or actions and are frequently produced for interaction-heavy products where defining the user's path is critical to understanding which features will support a smooth user experience.

WIREFRAMES. These illustrate the organization and information hierarchy of individual templates or pages. They may be used to show the general number of themes (sometimes called templates) that will be needed throughout a project. In other cases, they may be used to illustrate complex, unique pages.

DOUBLE THE STRATEGY

Content strategists work in-house and agency-side. You're lucky if both types are working on your project: they work in concert, but each strategist has a different set of responsibilities and focuses on a different set of concerns. Here, we outline content strategy from the agency side.

CONVERGENCE

More and more, content strategy and information architecture are converging. In our experience, the more they're integrated the better.

FIGURE 7.2
This illustration shows generic examples of each of three primary IA deliverables. Each provide different insights and explorations of the end product.

SITE MAP

USER FLOW

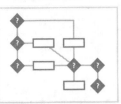

WIREFRAME

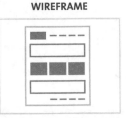

Project management checkpoint

Decide which of the deliverables above should be completed. The strategist and the project manager help the UXA and content teams determine what's possible and what's necessary to define the product for the rest of the team.

Don't let your team delve into detailed content strategy or information architecture at this point. The goal is to determine *just enough* to get an idea of what will be needed to complete the project. Keep people focused on high-level ideas and deliverables so the Research & Planning phase is most effective.

Outline the project requirements

Any project that contains a line of code must have a requirements definition (RD). So say we all.

The requirements definition articulates the end product in five key areas: definitions and conventions, features, production, technology, and security (Cheat Sheet 004). The goal is to brainstorm and decide on ways to use technology to meet the client's goals in the most efficient and effective ways. The itemized list creates an explanation and definition of the end product before it's built.

Beware: It's easy to lose your client at this point in the project. Make sure they understand *why* the requirements definition is important. Encourage your technical team to write the RD in a way that's accessible, and present it in an engaging way.

It's probably also easy to lose your reader at this point in the book. But, leadership, take note: the requirements definition document is what you will use to verify that your team did exactly what they said they would.

Requirements Definition

aka The Master List

The requirements definition (RD) is the scope authority for the project. It's a full inventory of features with precise descriptions of functionality.

MASTER LIST

OWNER:

TECH LEAD

CONTRIBUTORS:

PROJECT MANAGER

BACK-END DEVELOPER

USER EXPERIENCE ARCHITECT

PRODUCTION LEAD

TESTER

DESCRIPTION:

The RD captures the project in writing: It's a crucible for refining disparate ideas and converting them into actual deliverable features and establishing shared understanding of what the product will be.

The RD is a reference point for several expertise areas: it communicates to UXA what the key features must accomplish; it provides testers with the information they need to verify the end product; and it tells the project manager and the client how the project is being built.

First drafts are full of open questions, notes, and assumptions. These get whittled down and become declarations, examples, and details. By its completion, it captures the full project scope and clearly defines all features.

SPECIAL CONSIDERATIONS:

- The RD is the what, the production plan is the front-end how, and the development plan is the back-end how.

- The RD requires a lot of client input. Language and terminology should be client-oriented.

- The biggest risk with the RD isn't that it might be inaccurate, but that it might be missing something. A key focus of reviews should be identifying holes.

- The RD needs love, care, and good writing. Write it well.

LOCATION IN THE PROCESS:

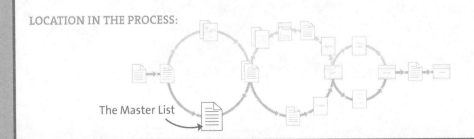

The Master List

DEFINITIONS AND CONVENTIONS. Establish a common project vernacular and define project-specific terms so there's no confusion when the team is having discussions. For instance: describing what exactly the word 'member' means when its used within project documentation ("a logged-in visitor to the site") or defining client-specific acronyms that everyone on the team needs to know about.

FEATURES. Features are the backbone of all products; they're the individual components that, when put together, make it interactive, that is, something users can actually interact with.

About each feature consider the associated variables, assumptions, and requirements; its purpose; and how it should work when users interact with it.

PRODUCTION. Outlines what production aspects affect how the product is executed.

Consider details like what browsers or programs need to support the site or app, required screen resolutions, and what parts of the product need to be print ready.

TECHNICAL. Often, technical points are framed as constraints. They outline what technology is being used and how is it being supported.

Consider what platform will be used, what features can be out-of-the-box versus custom, what kind of content needs to be supported and managed, and hosting requirements and specifications.

BE ACCESSIBLE

Account for any accessibility issues that may arise, like section 503 or ADA requirements.

THINK ABOUT: The mighty feature

Features are the "what" of the product. They must be clear, concise, and unambiguous in describing what users will be able to do with the product. The team relies on features to estimate costs and testers use features to verify the final product is fit for use. Good features are traceable through project documentation by their unique identifier and are defined in only one place. Finally, good features are always written in plain language. Vague features will cause questions during QA while overly specific features constrain the team in design.

SECURITY. What measures will be taken to secure the product or any data that will be collected, transmitted, or stored? Pay attention here! The client can get into a lot of trouble if data and security aren't handled properly.

Consider how data is being collected and stored, the security of financial transactions and whether the product must be PCI-DSS compliant, and whether all steps have been taken to mitigate fraud.

DRAFTS AND QUESTIONS. Requirements definitions are like schematics—they start out as rough sketches. Initial drafts will be peppered with questions. You'll then work with the client to address these questions as the requirements definition is reviewed. For a moderately-sized project, it's not unusual to make dozens of major updates to the document.

INVISIBLE ERRORS

Some of the hardest errors to find are errors of omission. First, make sure you've thought of the features necessary for every interaction. Then, as documents are created make sure features aren't accidentally omitted.

Project management checkpoint

The RD, while written in plain language, is written primarily by the technical team. Make sure that the technologists are itemizing *what* features will be built, not *how* they'll be built. It's easy to go down that path, but until the end product is finalized with the client—in the development approach—it's not necessary to think through the execution.

Always review new documents and deliverables against previously approved ones. Do this before *every* meeting and presentation with the client. You never want to give the client options that are outside scope or that conflict with what was presented earlier.

Effectively presenting documents to the client

As critical documents are presented to clients, frame information in ways that make sense to people who aren't used to reading through and visualizing this kind of information.

How to do this

USE PICTURES. Info-graphics, charts, or illustrations can help explain complex information. Do whatever it takes to help clients get their heads around all the details.

THINK ABOUT THE CLIENT AS A USER. Approach the client's experience as you would a user's experience with a website. The client is a user of your services—your ideas, assessments, and plans. The difference between an okay team and an excellent team is evidenced in how information is presented to the client.

READ THE ROOM. If the way you're presenting information doesn't seem to resonate with the client, change it up. Ask them what you and your team can do to make it more effective. Stress that you really need them to understand the information that is being presented to make sure the end product is as effective as it can be.

Project management checkpoint

Ultimately, the project manager spends a good portion of this project definition stage communicating information to the client. And it's frequently stuff that's abstract (information architecture) or technical (RD) which generally makes it harder to keep the client engaged. It's the project manager's and internal team's duty to communicate the information clearly.

Stress to the client that it's key they participate and make sure they know they have a critical role in determining the accuracy of the documents. The earlier the client recognizes something is missing, unnecessary, or incorrect, the better.

Recommend a solution

You've developed a smart strategy and UX brief, you've outlined high-level content strategy and information architecture, and enumerated a requirements definition that articulates the project in features and other technical requirements. Now it's time to figure out what can be done, how long it will take, and how much it's going to cost.

Where the beginning of Research & Planning is about possibility, the conclusion is about reality. Reality comes in the form of the final document in this phase, the development approach.

Estimate the project

Arriving at a realistic estimate is much easier once the high-level content strategy and information architecture is completed and the requirements definition is done and approved. With that, the team has the information they need to produce a reasonable estimate of the time and money it will take to build the end product.

Gather your entire team in a room to review the features, the content needs, and the overall volume of work. Use the individual team members' expertise to create the most accurate estimate of how much time it will take them to complete their own tasks.

Encourage them to be responsible to themselves and the client. In other words, don't radically underestimate time just to secure the project (but then fly through hours without completing the work) or radically overestimate just to cover your you-know-what (and potentially waste the client's money). Prepare estimates as a range that is both reasonable and accurate.

At Clockwork, we show a diagram to illustrate the relationship between key moments in the process and estimate accuracy (Figure 7.3). With this, the client sees that an estimate at this stage is far more accurate and realistic than any they've seen in prior documents. (And this isn't the first time the client sees this chart. We talk about it in the sales process as well.)

ESTIMATE AS A TEAM

Estimates are more accurate when the team sees the budget as something they contributed to instead of something that's forced on them. This increases their sense of personal investment in the project.

FIGURE 7.3
This diagram[5] shows how the estimate of cost range increases in accuracy as the project approaches completion. When the project first starts, the estimage range is wider than after Research & Planning, when the development approach plan is presented. While there's still a range, the expected costs are far more accurate.

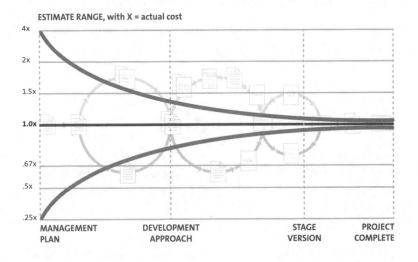

ESTIMATE RANGE, with X = actual cost

| | MANAGEMENT PLAN | DEVELOPMENT APPROACH | STAGE VERSION | PROJECT COMPLETE |

---

5   Adapted from a diagram published in Boehm, Barry et al., "Cost Models for Future Software Life Cycle Processes: COCOMO 2.0," *Annals of Software Engineering* 1 (1995): 57-94.

While there's still a range to our estimate, it's a lot smaller than it was when the project started. At this point, the client and the team have to agree on a number that may be a little too high, or a little too low, but which both are willing to live with.

Prepare the development approach

The development approach is the "Let's do this!" moment (Cheat Sheet 005). It outlines the final estimate for the project, and provides the context and reasoning behind the bottom line. It summarizes the team's final recommendations for the end product based on findings from Research & Planning.

How to do this

PROVIDE CONTEXT. At times, this can be a sobering dose of reality for the client. This document shows them exactly what things cost and how long they take. Anyone who's ever worked on any kind of project knows this can be tough information. Budget and timeline realities are often difficult to anticipate unless you're very familiar with the business (and this is the case with nearly every industry; think of how many car repair estimates have made you gasp!). That's exactly why you need to give the context and logic behind it all. While this doesn't make the bottom line any different, it makes it a little easier to understand.

THINK SCALABILITY. All projects come down to a balance of scope, budget, and time. Interactive products can, and should, evolve. Help clients see where and how their project can be broken into phases. Not every feature needs to be done in the first release. Compare the short-term budget and timeline against long-term objectives and needs. What needs to happen now? What can roll out later? And what will create the right foundation for the future additions?

Writing a thorough and helpful development approach and proposing phases will help the client see past the bottom line figure toward an overall project that's manageable.

Development Approach
aka The Agreement

The development approach summarizes the project scope, recommends an execution plan, and provides an estimate of how much it will cost to deliver.

OWNER:

PROJECT MANAGER

CONTRIBUTORS:

RELATIONSHIP MANAGER   ACCOUNT STRATEGIST   PRODUCTION LEAD   CREATIVE LEAD   TECH LEAD

DESCRIPTION:

The development approach is the plan and estimated cost to design and implement the agreed upon features. It's the result of many internal discussions in which content, features, technical requirements, and user experience architecture were outlined and estimated.

The development approach often recommends ways to fit the project goals into the original scope, time, and budget by presenting a phased approach or feature reduction. It helps clients make project decisions.

It takes a lot of back and forth to finalize the development approach. Once it's done, it becomes the contract for the rest of the project.

SPECIAL CONSIDERATIONS:

• Estimating is hard and takes practice. Use the development approach to track and analyze estimated versus actual costs.

• Consider having multiple team members present the development approach to the client tag team style. For instance, the tech lead should talk about platform options and features from the RD, the project manager should talk about dependencies, assumptions, timeline, etc.

LOCATION IN THE PROCESS:

The Agreement

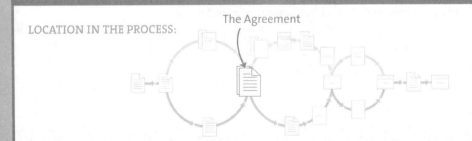

Present the development approach to the client

The primary function of the development approach is to communicate how much the end product will cost and when it can be done. It's crucial to present these hard facts with directness and care.

How to do this

COMMUNICATE THE TRUE SCOPE OF RECOMMENDATIONS. The development approach shows a clear breakdown of how each feature contributes to the overall scope. More importantly, it recommends ways to solve any problems caused by misalignment between budgets, timeline, and scope. Even the most daunting gaps between seemingly fixed details like scope and budget are received positively when the news is coupled with solid plans for moving forward.

EXPLAIN THE ASSUMPTIONS AND ESTIMATE. The assumptions and the final cost are the constraints that affect the scope of recommendations. These details help the client see the parameters that frame the project. Describe everything that's included in the estimate, and everything that's assumed about the project.

EMPHASIZE COLLABORATION. This document always changes between our first presentation and the final approval. Always. We open the conversation with the tone: "This is what we think should happen and why. What do *you* think?" This starts the conversation off on the right foot: Clients know we want the document to align with their vision and meet with their approval. We don't want clients to see the development approach as something that's being done *to* them, but as something that's being done *with* them.

At this point, three things could happen: The client and team solidify the development approach together and move forward with the project, the client could take the Research & Planning documents and shop around for other estimates, or the client may decide to postpone the project (or abandon it altogether). All of these are possibilities and realities of the industry.

ONLY INCLUDE WHAT'S POSSIBLE

Don't put a development approach that you can't deliver on in front of the client. Before you present the document, review resources and timing so the moment the client agrees to the project, tasks can start.

We encourage clients to seek other estimates based on our Research & Planning documents. We believe in our work and know that obtaining other estimates gives clients confidence and peace of mind. It's always productive to get a second (or even third!) opinion, and we never want clients to work with us if they have any doubt about the quality or objectivity of the partnership.

Takeaways

At first, it may seem like there isn't much happening during the project definition stage because the deliverables don't look like the end product. They're lists, tables, explanations, and reports. But they start to tell the full project story. When done well, these documents progressively clarify the project. They capture information and provide direction. As a whole, they sharpen the focus of the big picture. And that's pretty exciting.

The Research & Planning phase sets the project up for success. It ensures that the right thing is being produced in the right way, minimizes surprises, and maximizes collaboration. Furthermore, it creates buy-in among your team, both internally and client side. They all contributed to some part of the research process, so they've all had a hand in defining the work.

8

PROJECT PRODUCTION

Let the fun begin

This is when we start making stuff. Content! Design! Code! Whee!

In this chapter, we'll discuss

- The perfect project manager
- Front-end track: Pushing pixels
- Development track: Slinging code
- Convergence: Bringing the tracks together

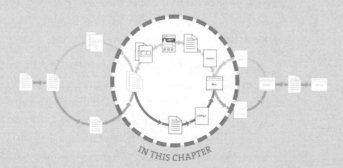

IN THIS CHAPTER

In the production stage, activity centers on delivering what was defined in the Research & Planning phase. Many tasks are being done concurrently, and there's a constant back and forth between people and departments. The potential for details to overlap, collide, or completely miss each other is in code-red zone.

If the Research & Planning phase was executed well, the team members should understand one another and also understand where the project is going. However, even with some of these variables ironed out and documented for easy reference, thinking, analyzing, ideating, and motivating are still critical. Executing a plan is more difficult than crafting one. So, buckle up.

Project management superstar!

Given the number of activities being done across the team, the production stage is particularly challenging for the project manager. Here's where you have the most moving parts and each expertise area actively producing work. And as each deliverable is completed, it has to align exactly with all the others. No pressure, though. It just has to align *exactly*.

The only way to ensure that the entire Production & Deployment phase rolls out smoothly is through excellent project management. The project manager must keep all the minutiae, people, and tasks aligned, while keeping the big picture in mind. Get into full stealth mode. Be everywhere. Know everything.

There are two important project management concepts we'll revisit throughout this stage.

RIGOR. How the team executes and reviews deliverables is key during this busy period. The purpose of all reviews is to push the whole team toward the best work possible. Effective reviews ensure that all perspectives are considered and that everyone is on the same page.

AGILITY. Changes are inevitable and necessary. The end product gets more and more defined as launch day approaches, so little—and sometimes very big— things get altered along the way. The trick is to accommodate these changes intelligently without the project jumping on a fast train to Crazytown. The later changes happen, the more money and time they cost (Figure 8.1). But refusing to accommodate changes won't make your client very happy. Find a balance.

COST OF CHANGE

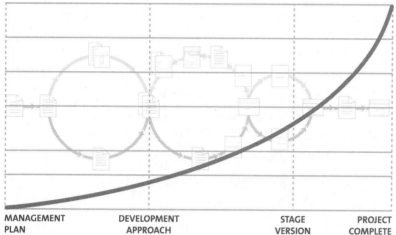

MANAGEMENT   DEVELOPMENT   STAGE   PROJECT
PLAN   APPROACH   VERSION   COMPLETE

FIGURE 8.1
This illustration shows
how the cost of change
increases as the project
moves from research to
deployment.[1]

Hold a production kickoff meeting

A production kickoff meeting with the internal team loops the existing members of the team back into the project, introduces any new team members, and gives everyone a chance to get acquainted with the scope and goals now that it's execution time.

There are three critical tasks that should happen in the re-kickoff meeting: document review, tactical thinking, and establishing timelines.

Review and update documents

Keeping all project documents up-to-date is essential to staying on track. Audit the approved documents to ensure that details are still accurate.

At the outset of the project, you assembled a core team. Now that you're shifting from Research & Planning to Production & Deployment, make sure the management plan still reflects the right team members and the communication plan as it's playing out. If anything has changed, edit and re-route to the internal and client teams.

"RE"-TASKS

Reviewing, recapping, and re-meeting ensure that the team is on track. And refamiliarizing the team with the documents and scope directly affects the accuracy of the proceeding work. The cost of doing this early on pays off in having fewer "re"s later— like reworking, revising, or regretting.

---

1   This diagram is adapted from Barry Boehm's findings published in *Software Engineering Economics* (Prentice Hall, 1981).

After the approval of the development approach, the team knows the exact scope of the project. Update the requirements definition to reflect what's actually being built. The RD should itemize only the features that were approved; remember, it's the written version of the final end product.

Think tactically about next steps

SPOTTING ROADBLOCKS

Listen for team members saying things like, "I can't start that until..."

Ultimately, your team has to walk away from this meeting with something to do and a clear idea of how and when to do it. To get the team to that point, discuss what needs to happen and in what order.

To create the best tactical plans, ask yourself:

- What tasks can we start now? What should be done in the short-term to make the long-term milestones achievable?

- Which tasks cross expertise areas, and thus need to be done in a specific order?

- What features or tasks should be done in an iterative style (create, review, refine, review, and so on) and which ones should be done in a waterfall style (sequentially)?

Establish timelines

Once the deadline is known, short-term and long-term milestones must be determined. The project manager leads this task, but setting milestones as a team is the most effective way to set realistic time frames, and ensure that team members feel a sense of control over what they're being asked to do.

TIP: Show, don't tell

When clients push for an aggressive schedule, use the timeline to show them how quickly they will have to provide assets and approvals. At times, this gets them to ease up, because while they don't necessarily understand how long things take in the interactive industry, they do understand how long things take in theirs ("Oh no, we'll never get approval in two business days. Yes, let's push out the due date."). Overly aggressive timelines affect everyone.

Here's how to build a useful timeline:

GET ONLY AS DETAILED AS NECESSARY. Aim for a balance between rigor and agility. This doesn't mean fly by the seat of your pants; it means don't over-complicate things.

> *YEAH, BUT…What about detailed work breakdowns, dependencies, and durations? How am I supposed to make a Gantt chart out of this?!*

> *GLAD YOU ASKED…This is, admittedly, a lean approach to timeline production. But it works. The best timelines are detailed enough to ensure that disparate elements are well orchestrated, but not so detailed that any change requires hours of work to reconfigure. The key is to provide guidance about timing and expectations for due dates, and to let the people on your team make good decisions within those parameters. If the only person on the team who can understand or update the timeline is the project manager—it's too complicated.*

ASK FOR INPUT. People work better when they have a say in managing their time. Use the team's experience to determine reasonable durations for tasks. They have the best handle on how much time it takes to do their work.

BE REALISTIC. Be responsible to your team and the client when determining timelines. Things like other projects, sick days, and delays will happen, so pro-actively account for them. If the client pushes for a shorter project calendar, explain why you need the time you do or resources you require. Be clear, but also be collaborative. Make sure they know you're trying to work *with* them to get the best product in the best time.

Coordinate information among your team

Elements within interactive projects are ridiculously interconnected; nearly every detail has some effect on another area. As you move through the entire Production & Deployment phase, there are *a lot* of deliverables produced by *many* people. Because deliverables have to align exactly, you will find yourself constantly coordinating information among your internal team.

Successfully reviewing the deliverables is crucial to achieving full-team collaboration and engagement as well as accuracy. We hold two types of review meetings: departmental and internal.

IMPORTANT DATES

Two critical milestones to define early on are when you expect clients to review and to approve things.

LITTLE WHITE LIES

It's tempting to give your team earlier deadlines to create "extra" time—like, tell them Monday when you don't really need it until Tuesday. Be careful with that; if the team catches on they'll stop following the deadlines you give and assume they have more time hidden.

SHARE RESOURCES

In companies with more than one project manager, team members may have conflicting deadlines. When those situations arise, don't burden team members with the job of figuring out which project is more important. Project managers should negotiate resources, set priorities, and, if necessary, renegotiate deadlines.

DEPARTMENTAL REVIEWS are performed among people within a single expertise area and are designed to push each other to do better work. As a group these people examine discipline-specific work across the company's projects. The purpose is to evaluate the deliverable against company standards.

INTERNAL TEAM REVIEWS involve the project team, which includes a cross-section of disciplines. Team members review the work to ensure that it meets the project standards and goals. Internal reviews are about thoughtful approvals and careful evaluation.

How to have successful review meetings

AGENDA INPUT

Other team members should be able to contribute to the agenda. Send out an email in advance and ask if anyone has points they want to address. That way, people won't feel like they're hijacking the meeting if they have something they need to talk about.

Reviews are especially critical in the production stage because the further along a project gets the more expensive it is to make changes. People hate meetings, but they aren't the problem—*mismanaged* meetings are. Don't let them happen!

ROUTE DOCUMENTS. Send out all deliverables for advance review.

HAVE A CLEAR MEETING OWNER. A single person should create an agenda and lead the review (cue: project manager.)

USE THE DOCUMENT TO GUIDE THE REVIEW. But, please, don't *read* the deliverable out loud. There's nothing more painful than sitting through a dramatic reading of project documentation.

The project manager and strategist should take on the role of client when reviewing the team's work. Have team members present their work at the internal reviews. If nothing else, it's a good dress rehearsal for the client meeting.

Front-end: Pushing pixels

As we mentioned in Chapter 7, "Project Definition," front-end doesn't come before back-end, but books are linear and we had to start somewhere! As before, things are happening concurrently and collaboratively.

Finish the content strategy and information architecture

In the Research & Planning phase, the high-level content strategy and information architecture outlined what kind of work was *likely* going to be required. Now that we know what's being built (from the development approach), the team looks more closely at what *actually* needs to be done to create a productive, meaningful, and successful experience for the end user (Cheat Sheet 006).

Think of this as a gap analysis: You have rough plans from the Research & Planning phase and you know the end product, so now you determine what has to happen to turn the plans into a usable thing. The project type and scope determine the exact deliverables; some products may need very specific documents, while others may have more flexibility.

Fine-tuning content strategy

Most projects require at least one of three core content strategy deliverables: a content audit, a content matrix, and content guidelines.

The **content audit**, initially started in the Research & Planning phase, outlines existing content. A **content matrix** lists pieces of content that need to be produced and the plan for executing it. Finally, **content guidelines** articulate the necessary information to guide the creation of content.

Successful detailed content strategy deliverables will:

- Isolate what's needed now and what will be needed in the future to maintain the product and continue achieving goals.

- Think about who is creating content, and how it will be managed.

- Determine how content will be developed, initiate a copy deck, and assign responsibility to whoever will be completing it.

CONTENT NEVER STOPS

Content development is ongoing. After launch, content will continue to be created, published, edited, and removed from nearly every product you make. Content strategy ensures that this is planned for.

Detailed Content Strategy & Information
Architecture aka The Blueprint

Detailed content strategy and information architecture define and communicate the organization of content and interactive behavior of the product at the page level.

OWNERS:

USER EXPERIENCE
ARCHITECT

CONTENT STRATEGIST

CONTRIBUTORS:

PRODUCTION
LEAD

ACCOUNT
STRATEGIST

CREATIVE LEAD

TECH LEAD

DESCRIPTION:

Detailed content strategy and IA deliverables create a robust blueprint referenced by all expertise areas. They pick up where high level deliverables left off and outline exact content and user interactions that make up the final product. Together they show the design and front-end development teams what's needed to create a productive user experience.

The team finishes the content audit started in planning, and completes a content matrix and content guidelines. These ensure that current and future content align with project goals. Detailed IA thoroughly accounts for all features and functionality in wireframes and verifies that all user interactions have been accounted for and given appropriate emphasis and consideration.

SPECIAL CONSIDERATIONS:

• The user experience architect must align specific content and interactions with the overall strategic goals and specific features.

• Because IA is visual in nature, it can be useful for gathering early usability feedback before features are built.

• Several iterations are typically needed before everything is approved.

• Remember to cross-reference these docs with the RD.

LOCATION IN THE PROCESS:

The Blueprint

Finalizing information architecture

First, review any deliverables produced in the Research & Planning phase to assess their accuracy. Make edits to get your documents up to date. Then, dig deeper. This will mean going into more detail within the documents you have as well as possibly creating more. As with the high-level work, the deliverables vary depending on the project. As the project manager, work with the UXA team to think about exactly what needs to be outlined to organize and hierarchize information appropriately.

Effective IA will:

- Outline how the user interacts with each functional element (What happens when it works? How are errors dealt with?).

- Take into account any standard conventions that may dictate IA, for example, whether there are product-, platform- or brand-specific interfaces and content that should be considered.

- Examine which interactions need further elaboration for design.

- Determine detailed content features and information hierarchy.

Project management checkpoint

RIGOROUS REVIEW. Internal team reviews for content and IA are absolutely critical. Both of these disciplines—and their deliverables—affect so many parts of the end product that all eyes must see what they're delivering.

Help your team have effective review sessions. Ensure that content needs are accounted for throughout the IA and RD. As development progresses, make sure the development team pays close attention to how their features align with IA.

ACCOMMODATING AGILITY. As the project progresses, the client sees more tangible versions of their product and they start to better understand what they need and want. For example, seeing a wireframe can clarify a feature in a way that makes more sense than that same feature described in the RD. These realizations happen a lot at the detailed content strategy and IA stage. And they may change the direction of some features. If changes occur, consult with other team members about scope impact, and edit other documents or deliverables that may be impacted.

COMPARE IA AND RD

It's easy for IA and RD to get out of alignment, so make sure the two teams are looking closely at each other's deliverables. Many a project team has been foiled by a feature sneaking into the IA that wasn't in the RD. It's best if the two documents cross-reference each other using feature numbers (for the RD) and page numbers (for the IA).

Refine creative ideas

The road leading to a final design varies based on a few factors: the size and duration of the project, the complexity of the user interaction, the intricacy of client brand standards, and the size of the project team (and within that, the design team).

To begin, designers should reference the strategy and user experience (UX) brief, especially the creative considerations section. Then, they refine.

Align with the client

DESIGN MAKES A DIFFERENCE

Good design serves the goals, prioritizes information according to end user and business needs, and pushes the product from usable to enjoyable.

One of the biggest challenges with design is making sure that the design team understands what the client wants from a visual standpoint. Design goals are often written as adjectives within the strategy and UX brief, leaving it open for interpretation. For example, "Clean and Modern" can mean one thing to one person and something completely different to another. Here are some helpful exercises to make sure you're on the same page.

INSPIRATION SITES. Ask the client to identify web sites that they like from a design standpoint, and more importantly sites that capture the desired look and feel. Ideally, the designer can then hear first hand what the client likes and dislikes about each.

STYLE GUIDES. Many clients have an existing style guide or brand guide, and in those cases it is very important to walk through this document together. When one does not exist, it is often very helpful to pull together a condensed version, reiterating the things you know about an existing brand.

MOODBOARDS. Moodboards bring together different design elements, everything from website screenshots to photography and typography samples, to evoke a particular feeling or mood. You may get buy-in of an overall direction, or you may get specific feedback about individual elements; either way it's helpful to make sure you and the client are on the same page.

THINK ABOUT: Sharing your process

Many clients enjoy seeing the creative process, and it can often lead to a more effective design time if you get feedback along the way. For example, a client might call out a sketch that they really like or they might catch something that they don't like. This can save a lot of time. It also has the added benefit of getting early buy-in from the client, increasing the chances that the concept presentation will be successful.

Explore conceptual models

Once you have a good sense of what the client wants from a look and feel standpoint, it's time to explore a range of approaches to execute. Conceptual models help provide structure to this brainstorming activity and push the designer to explore multiple solutions. Some of the more common conceptual models are described below.[2]

SPECTRUMS. A spectrum (Figure 8.2) works well when you're exploring two opposing approaches. For example, you might want to sketch one layout that is close to the client's brand and one that pushes the brand.

2X2S. A 2x2 uses two sets of adjectives along axes to create a quadrant of ideas. Examples include, Polished/Authentic and Close to brand/Push the brand. The result would be a quadrant with the four possible combinations of those attributes.

GRIDS. A grid is useful when you have more than two spectrums to explore and can be used to generate an almost infinite number of layout options.

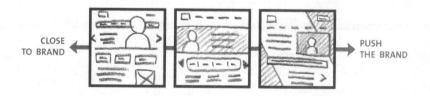

CLOSE
TO BRAND

PUSH
THE BRAND

FIGURE 8.2
This graphic shows an example of a spectrum drawing. More complex versions of the spectrum concept are 2x2s and grids. The axis values for any concept model should be attributes that help the team find a visual solution.

2 The conceptual models presented here are taken from Leah Buley's work, found at http://www.adaptivepath.com/ideas/d071508.

Design Concepts
aka Painting with Pixels

Design concepts are mockups of the prominent screens in the end product.

OWNER:

DESIGNER

CONTRIBUTORS:

CREATIVE LEAD

USER EXPERIENCE
ARCHITECT

CONTENT
STRATEGIST

DESCRIPTION:

Design concepts bring together information architecture and all visual exploration work (moodboards, concept sketches, etc.) into mockups that closely mimic the final product. They allow the client to see how the final product will look and ensure everyone is aligned on visual direction.

Typically two or three concepts are presented to the client, exploring a range of visual styles as well as options for how to approach the treatment of content through photography and typography.

SPECIAL CONSIDERATIONS:

• Give the internal team a chance to weigh in on interactions, functionality, and content before presenting to the client.

• When presenting design, reference project goals and explain how design elements achieve those goals.

• Think about ways to emulate the final product environment. For example, you may want to have laptops, tablets, and/or mobile devices available.

• When possible use real or close-to-real content in mockups.

LOCATION IN THE PROCESS:

Painting with Pixels

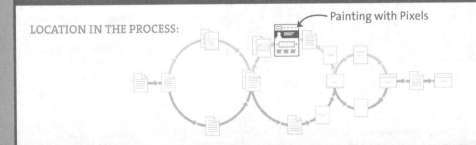

THINK ABOUT: Design and functionality

In interactive projects, design implies functionality. In other words, the design must indicate which elements have interactive properties, suggest the outcome of interacting with those elements, and deliver on that promise to the end user. When something looks like a link to another web page but behaves like a "Download PDF" button, a promise has been broken.

Consider how interactions can be most effectively communicated in design concepts. This depends on the complexity of the project, the team's skills, and the availble time and budget. Encourage the team to collaborate and get creative. A static concept in Photoshop might do the trick, but it doesn't have to be the only option. Keynote for iPad can be used to simulate iOS transitions; Flash can simulate site scrolling effects; InVision, OmniGraffle, and ProtoShare can create lo-fi page layouts and linking.

Design and user experience are quickly moving toward a prototyping and "design in the browser" model. Try it!

Create design concepts

The first set of concepts is usually based on one screen (which one is up to the team but, for a website project, it's typically the homepage). These concepts introduce the design motifs and overall feel of the product (Cheat Sheet 007). They take into account the brand standards, and apply these to the functionality, content, and architecture that have been established in the IA. The number of unique design concepts presented depends on timing and budget, but three is the magic number.

Project management checkpoint

RIGOROUS REVIEW. Both departmental and internal reviews of design concepts are necessary. The team needs these to ensure this highly-charged deliverable is as polished as it can be.

In internal reviews, let everyone weigh in on design. Disallow comments like, "I don't really like blue," but encourage insight, questions, and additional ideas from expertise areas, such as, "What if the client wants to put photos over there?" or "Where is the login area?" or "We could take that idea a step further with JavaScript."

START WITH COMPLEX

On a content- or interaction-heavy site, encourage the team to develop concepts for a very complex page (versus the homepage or the first screen of an app). This ensures that, from the beginning, the design can accommodate the complex interactions required or handle the amount of content.

PRESENT UP

Design department reviews are frequently reviews with a creative or art director. Share designs with them to ensure the concept is pushed to be the best it can be.

SHOW VARIATIONS

Show how the design changes in liquid layouts, responsive layouts or full width and/or height sections of the layout or at different screen resolutions.

Think like the client when reviewing concepts and work with the design team on perfecting what's presented. Ensure that the team is anticipating the client's reaction and concerns, gathering data to support design decisions, and aligning the concepts with all project facts.

Presenting design to clients

Presenting design concepts can be a very charged moment for the project. People connect emotionally with design: they often have personal, subjective reactions to it and frequently have strong opinions. Moreover, this is the first time when the client sees their vision in something that feels real. Thoughtful planning and collaborative work creates a productive environment.

Think about how to make it effective for the client to give good feedback and your internal team to receive good feedback.

SELL YOUR THINKING. Go through the reasons and rationales for the decisions you made and the conclusions you came to. Share the logic or the experience your team went through to get to concepts. These are solutions, not just designs. ("Your target audiences are very specific, and very different, so we wanted to make a screen that was clearly divided between users while still maintaining the overall feel of the brand.")

EXTERNALIZE THE DEBATE. Don't make it about one person's preference or opinion versus another's. Center the conversation on the goals, strategies, requirements, and restrictions that were laid out in the Research & Planning phase. Refer back to the documents and decisions that the project is built on, and that support the designs. ("According to the research, the number one thing users want is quick access to sign-in. That's why we placed it centrally on the main page.")

ASK FOR PROBLEMS, NOT SOLUTIONS. Encourage clients to focus on what they like or don't like, not how to solve it. The classic example is the "make the logo bigger" conversation. When feedback becomes direction, try to ask questions that lead back to the underlying issue. "Okay, I wrote that you'd like the logo bigger in our meeting notes. Are you suggesting that because the branding just doesn't feel strong enough?" Digging into the driving factors helps to position your team as critical thinkers and problem solvers, not just order takers. (But, sometimes you will have to just make the logo bigger.)

Project management checkpoint

Because design can be so emotional, personal, and subjective, projects can get mired in extensive rounds of revisions. Scope alert!

Keep the client focused on making decisions and moving forward. Gentle reminders about due dates for final feedback or the number of revisions that are in scope can help focus attention and encourage approvals.

As the design team receives the feedback, remember that it can be difficult to hear. Help translate feedback into constructive criticism.

FOCUS THE FEEDBACK

Not everything about the design has to be "final"— things like headline styles and colors can easily be revised after production (or even launch). If the client is fixating on details that can be easily changed later, help them focus on what essentials need to be approved for the project to move forward.

Moving from design to front-end development

Where the documents in Research & Planning were foundation for the project, plans in the Production & Deployment phase are discipline-specific. The project comes into clearer shape as the front-end development team uses the design concepts to create clickable interfaces that the end user can interact with (in cases where design prototypes were created, front-end development may be taking those to a more finished, functional state).

The deliverables in this stage all feed into the first, full-sized example of the end product: the development version.

Create the production plan

Front-end development brings design and functionality together into an interface that can be used intelligently and easily by users. This is an important junction of design, back-end development, and content.

As the planning deliverable for the front-end development team, the production plan walks through every feature and design element to figure out the best way to build it (Cheat Sheet 008).

The production plan is a very technical document read mostly by the front-end developers and tech leads; it's rarely presented to the client. (Of course, it's available if they want to see it, but it probably won't be very meaningful.)

PUSHING
THE PIXELS

Production Plan

aka The Screenplay

The production plan defines all production tasks necessary to accomplish the list of requirements itemized in the information architecture and requirements definition.

OWNER:

PRODUCTION LEAD

CONTRIBUTORS:

FRONT-END
DEVELOPER

USER EXPERIENCE
ARCHITECT

TECH LEAD

CREATIVE LEAD

DESCRIPTION:

The production plan facilitates a thoughtful approach to front-end development tasks. It provides recommendations, definitions, and plans to build the features and functionality listed in the RD, UXA, and design.

As a planning document, the production plan communicates how to build the final product. It defines development environments, outlines how features and interactions will be completed, and considers technical and creative details. Outlining tasks makes it easy to assess remaining work, enables problem solving, and brings to light any dependencies or open questions.

This document is a road map for the front-end developers: It helps them work efficiently and empowers them to resolve obstacles before they become bigger issues.

SPECIAL CONSIDERATIONS:

• The RD is the what, the production plan is the front-end how, and the development plan is the back-end how.

• Front-end development should work closely with designers to ensure that all design details are clearly articulated.

• All tasks should align with specific features in UXA, the RD, and design concepts.

• Think about individual front-end developers' levels of expertise when outlining tasks; different developers will need different information.

LOCATION IN THE PROCESS:

The Screenplay

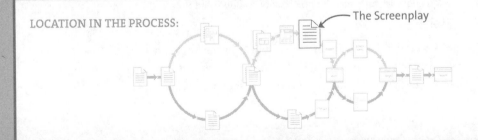

Align expertise areas

Front-end development converges with three expertise areas: content, design, and back-end development. It's critical that as the front-end team moves forward, they're aligned with the work and direction within those disciplines.

CONTENT. Final production deliverables articulate what content is needed and where it's needed, ensuring that all content in the end product, as it's being built, aligns with the needs and plans of the content strategists. As the product is finalized, you don't want a last minute rush to obtain content for easily-overlooked areas of the product.

DESIGN. The front-end developer's role is to bring the design to life, so she needs to know *exactly* what the designer has in mind with the concept. Both design and front-end developers are responsible for a successful handoff. Design should be sure they've made the details clear and front-end developers need to make sure they're getting everything they need.

BACK-END DEVELOPMENT. Front- and back-end teams have to coordinate when and how they want to hand work back and forth. The two teams should work together to plan the order in which features are handed off. The goal is to keep work moving through each discipline's workflow without getting hung up. As a project manager, you don't want either team waiting on the other.

IDENTIFY ROADBLOCKS

Tasks can get held up between front-end development and back-end development. The production plan is a perfect place for the front-end team to identify what tasks are being blocked, or will likely be blocked, by back-end development.

Front-end development vs. back-end development

It's not easy to *see* the difference between front-end and back-end work because they're well integrated in the end product.

FRONT-END DEVELOPERS produce code that powers the elements of the end product that users see and interact with. This means developing screens, forms, and interactive elements, such as what happens when a user clicks something. Front-end developers make sure elements are presented in a usable way.

BACK-END DEVELOPERS produce code to power the mostly behind-the-scenes, functional elements of a product, such as how user-entered data is passed from a web page into a database. Back-end developers make sure the product works.

Remember what we said earlier about everything being ridiculously interconnected? This is the kind of stuff we were talking about.

Produce themes

What we call themes are sometimes referred to as templates, but that just sounds so restrictive. And they really shouldn't be restrictive, so we're sticking with themes (Cheat Sheet 009). If the design concepts were the first glance at what the end product will look like, the themes are the first glance at what the end product will feel like to the user.

The goal is to balance design consistency with content flexibility and layout variation. The design concepts are adopted and riffed on, and the IA guides the layouts. The creative team shouldn't be threatened by this; they don't have to dictate every pixel. On the other hand, front-end developers shouldn't take this as carte blanche to do their own thing. The design team is going to be looking at this again later!

THEME ROULETTE

Pick a random page from the content matrix and ask: How would this page work with the available themes?

Themes provide the master structure for any given page. For example, "internal two-column theme" may be used a number of times, but what appears on the actual screens will change. Individual pieces of content—images, blog entry, headline, body copy—create the individualization necessary for the product to make sense. That's what allows the pages or screens to feel unique and appropriate for that page, while still giving users a predictable experience.

Project management checkpoint

The project manager's role during this production period is ensuring that each team has all the information needed to keep the project moving forward. Any constraints or dependencies should be flagged early on and managed between the project manager and the team.

The front-end developer will likely be less familiar with the project than those who've been intimately involved since Research & Planning. Check in with the front-end developer right around the design handoff; often she'll have questions that a project manager can answer off the top of her head. Make it as easy as possible for them to jump in and start work.

Themes

aka Making It Click

Themes translate design concepts, user experience architecture, and features into flexible templates that comprise the fully functioning end product.

OWNER:

FRONT-END DEVELOPER

CONTRIBUTORS:

PRODUCTION
LEAD

BACK-END
DEVELOPER

USER EXPERIENCE
ARCHITECT

DESCRIPTION:

Themes are templates that create the fully-developed end product. They're consistent and flexible iterations of the design concept and they dictate how users interact with features and what everything actually looks like.

Themes are the intersection of content, design, user experience, and functionality, and they create a predictable interface for the user. They make the end product look good and work well with content of varying types and lengths, provide structure and layouts for all screens within the product, and enable easy use and management of content regardless of technical features.

As the foundation of the end product, they must be produced with solid code that stands the test of time.

SPECIAL CONSIDERATIONS:

• All expertise areas review the themes because they affect all elements: features, content, and design.

• Consider all browsers, devices, search engines, printers, social media sharing, operating systems, connection/rendering speeds, and any other delivery methods when producing themes.

LOCATION IN THE PROCESS:

Making It Click

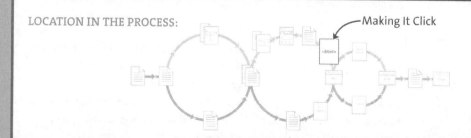

Back-end: Slinging code

Back-end development builds the engine that makes the end product run. And this requires just as much thinking as it does action.

Deliver a development plan

START THE TEST PLAN

Testers should start writing the test plan now. As developers work through features, the testers can simultaneously work on how to test those features. The two groups will end up challenging each other to refine and implement the features.

As the planning deliverable for the back-end development team, the development plan details how each feature and functional element will be built (Cheat Sheet 010). It's for developers, by developers.

The primary purpose of this plan is to maximize foresight and minimize missteps. The development team should mentally walk through the code that has to be written and what exactly needs to be done. Our team often sits together and goes through the requirements, one feature at a time, and outlines a plan for every item. Measure twice, cut once.

This document evolves and changes while each feature gets fully outlined. Some initial coding may begin before it's officially approved, but most of the development will start once it's done.

In many ways, this is a direct parallel to the front-end production plan: it's a step-by-step plan, a technical document used primarily by developers, and it's rarely presented to the client. (Like the production plan, it's available to clients if they want to see it, but probably won't be very meaningful.)

Project management checkpoint

RIGOROUS REVIEW. Client reviews are generally nonexistent when it comes to the development plan. But departmental reviews are essential. Most project team members don't know enough about development to provide useful feedback here, but other developers can recognize if there's something wrong or missing.

The project manager isn't necessarily directly participating in the creation of the development plan, but as with other expertise area documents, she is ensuring that it's getting done in an efficient manner, liaising with the client when there are questions, and helping the development team prioritize and forecast the plan. She's communicating due dates and expectations, and—when necessary—raising red flags to the client.

WRITING
THE CODE

Development Plan

aka The Manual

The development plan provides technical explanations of how each requirement from the requirements definition will be implemented in software.

OWNER:

BACK-END DEVELOPER

CONTRIBUTORS:

TECH LEAD

DESCRIPTION:

The development plan is the path that takes you from a list of features to a working product. To create the plan, all requirements are evaluated, discussed, and outlined, and then a development direction is established for each.

Features require thoughtful planning. Each feature should be fully articulated in a thorough description of how it will function. Mapping requirements to specific features, and features to itemized tasks puts the team a few steps ahead of the programming necessary to build the complete end product.

The goal is to understand how the feature will take shape before code is written. Writing code based on a well-vetted development plan is more efficient than problem-solving while developing.

SPECIAL CONSIDERATIONS:

- The RD is the what, the production plan is the front-end how, and the development plan is the back-end how.

- All team members must be able to understand this document, especially any new personnel that may be brought onto a project after production has kicked off.

- Map each feature in the RD to specific tasks to serve as a requirements checklist. Errors of omission are the hardest to spot!

- Include brief descriptions of how any existing structures will be used.

LOCATION IN THE PROCESS:

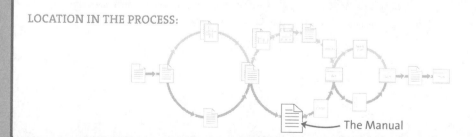

The Manual

Code: it makes things work

Code is the foundation of interactive work (Cheat Sheet 011). Code is

- A collection of content used in various capacities to make the end product work. It's the stuff that makes everything from the search feature to the navigation menu function. Every piece of the end product that *does something* is powered by code.

- A generic term that includes numerous languages. It's best described as the engine that powers all digital things. If the end product were a car, code would be all the stuff under the hood: It's wildly varied but similar in that it all works together to make the car go.

Code isn't completed in one chunk and handed off. It's a living part of the product that is worked on over the course of the Production & Deployment phase.

It's tricky for most nondevelopers to understand code. For this reason, code isn't typically shown to the client. Like the development plan, they are more than welcome to see and review it, but most won't. An exception would be a client with an extensive IT team that has an interest in auditing or testing your work.

Custom code vs. existing software

On interactive projects, there are two broad categories of code that contribute to how code is developed: custom and off the shelf. On some projects, you'll build everything from scratch, on others you'll use existing software out of the box, and at other times you'll use a combination. The pros and cons should be well articulated and well considered.

CUSTOM CODE. Custom code is developed specifically for the project. While custom usually means more work, it can be a good option if the client wants to "own" the work. The con is that once the client has custom code, they (or their development partner) are responsible for maintaining and updating that code (as opposed to getting regular upgrades from existing software).

Code

aka The Engine

Code powers the end product and ensures it operates in accordance with the user experience architecture and technical requirements.

OWNER:

BACK-END DEVELOPER

CONTRIBUTORS:

FRONT-END DEVELOPER   TECH LEAD   PRODUCTION LEAD   TESTER

DESCRIPTION:

Code ensures that every user action produces the desired effect by translating features from the requirements definition into computer language. Computers require all features to be programmed in unambiguous detail. When code runs correctly, no one notices it; when it fails, it's the only thing that's noticed.

High quality code is the result of developers working with stable requirements, adequate planning, and sufficient time. It's detrimental for code—and the end product—to be rushed or changed frequently due to edits to the requirements or IA.

Where quality code is relatively easy to understand and maintain, bad code is so inscrutable that minor changes become big productions and updates require complete rewrites.

SPECIAL CONSIDERATIONS:

- Developers need lengths of uninterrupted time to produce quality code.

- Code reviews are a simple and proven way to reduce bugs.

- With that in mind: No code is bug free. Schedule and plan for bugs.

- Adding developers to reduce development time doesn't work. More developers will finish faster only when tasks are not interrelated. In other words, nine women can't have a baby in one month.

LOCATION IN THE PROCESS:

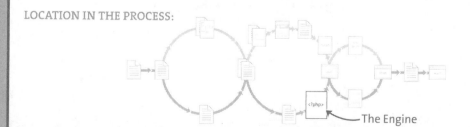

The Engine

EXISTING SOFTWARE. Existing software includes programs that you purchase or subscribe to that provide already-written code and functionality. The pro is a lot of work has already been done and time and budget can be focused on client-specific cusomizations. The con can be limitations in customizability or the long-term reliance on a third-party product or partner.

The important thing to note here is that the client has to understand the distinction, and the team has to recommend the best choice (custom vs. existing) within time and budget. You don't want the client asking to fine-tune something that can't be customized. At the same time, you don't want your team to spend valuable time (and money) reinventing the wheel.

Project management checkpoint

RIGOROUS REVIEWS. Departmental reviews are *vital* when it comes to code. This allows other developers to constructively review the project team's work, make recommendations, and ensure that the quality of the code is high.

WEEKLY STATUSES

The production phase is chaotic—there's no way around that—but status updates get everyone on the same page and freeze everything for just a moment so you can see all the moving parts statically (or at least in slow motion).

ACCOMMODATING AGILITY. Listen closely for clues about changes as code is developed. Ask questions to ensure that the developers are keeping IA, content, design, and front-end development aligned and informed. Encourage everyone to keep an eye on any details that affect other teams and their work. A slight change to how a feature is coded may mean a slight change to what content is needed and what buttons are created. This isn't the end of world if it gets communicated right away, but further down the line it may cost more to fix.

As usual, the project manager does a lot of communicating, reacting, observing, and planning to make sure things are moving along exactly as they should. She facilitates the meetings that ensure code is being reviewed, she liaises with the production team to make sure that code is being handed off for front-end development in the manner that's expected, and she follows up with the development team to check that file versioning and storage is being handled as efficiently. Remember, ninja: Be *everywhere*.

THINK ABOUT: Acronyms

Interactive is riddled with acronyms and abbreviations for languages, file types, and technology. Keep your ears open for things like AJAX, CSS, HTML, iOS, JS, MySQL, .NET, PNG, PSD, SSL, SQL and many more. If you don't know what an acronym means, look it up. The more you know, the better you'll understand the interrelationships between tasks, how projects develop, and how to explain it all to your clients.

Front-end and back-end converging

What do IA, content, production, and development look like when they all come together? Hopefully something close to the envisioned end product!

Build a development version

The development version is first draft of the end product (Cheat Sheet 012). But it's only for the internal team (the client will see their version in the next stage). Think of this as the technical rehearsal, the first place where the front-end and back-end tracks' work are united. It's a glimpse at how the end product will look, feel, and operate when it's complete.

Work is done simultaneously and uploads are happening frequently. As each team member completes work, they upload it to the development version. It's an in-progress version that is constantly changing. In this respect, there isn't a *singular* development version. There are many iterations as work is edited and updated again and again.

And because it's a work-in-progress, it's often unstable and full of gaps—which is why the client doesn't look at it. In the next chapter, we'll discuss how to get from the internal development version to a client-ready stage version.

CHEAT SHEET 012

Development Version

aka The Work in Progress

The development version of a site is the construction site used by the team when building features of a project.

OWNERS:

FRONT-END DEVELOPER   BACK-END DEVELOPER

CONTRIBUTORS:

TESTER   TECH LEAD   PRODUCTION LEAD

DESCRIPTION:

The development version is what individual developers—both front-end and back-end—use to test, tweak, and finalize features. It's an in-progress version of the end product onto which independent developers' work is brought together for the internal team to assess functionality. It's like a technical rehearsal before the stage version.

Often, the development version will not be wholly functional because work is constantly being edited and uploaded. Moreover, completing individual features rarely requires a completely built-out product.

Because the development version is always under construction, it isn't stable or predictable. For this reason, it's for the internal team's eyes only.

SPECIAL CONSIDERATIONS:

• Testers should test features on development versions before they are deployed on the stage versions.

• Mimic the live version server configuration as closely as possible when creating the development version.

LOCATION IN THE PROCESS:

The Work in Progress

Takeaways

The production stage is about maintaining a delicate balance of all the project factors: individuals and expertise areas, planning and executing, and initial ideas and new developments.

All of this happens while you're barreling toward the finish line. And by the end, the team has something that's starting to resemble the end product.

The project manager manages like a maniac during this stage. She reviews, assesses, analyzes, thinks, communicates, and has countless—but well-managed—meetings. She keeps everyone on the same page, monitors the project's progress, aligns teams and deliverables, and does it all with a smile.

9

PROJECT STAGING

Feedback and fine-tuning

The stage version is the client's first glimpse at the full, working product that they've been waiting for. It's an exciting time.

In this chapter, we'll discuss

- Preparation: Finishing touches and finalizing content
- Testing: Fine-tuning the machine
- Convergence: Presenting the work to the client

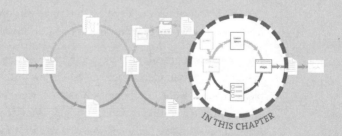

IN THIS CHAPTER

Where the production stage was about coordinating tasks and people, the stage stage (wait, what?) is about communicating, translating, and motivating. The project manager must be on top of his liaising game, ensuring that team members understand one another as well as the project requirements during these last critical steps to launch.

Prepare the finishing touches

The development version contains all the front- and back-end work that the team has produced throughout the project. Now, all that work moves to a client-friendly stage version for review and approval. And from there, it becomes the live version.

Define the stage version

What the stage version looks like and the number of times it's reviewed depends on three factors: the size of the project, the client's comfort level with interactive products, and the client's level of engagement with the project. We use *stage* to refer to any version of the end product that's ready for the client to review.

For the sake of simplicity, the diagram of our process in Chapter 5 shows a single, linear path from development to stage version to live version (Figure 5.1). But there doesn't have to be—and in most cases there shouldn't be—only one big reveal. The client can monitor progress, and your team can receive intermittent feedback, by reviewing the stage version throughout the project.

On a small four- to six-week project, this stage version is likely a single, launch-ready version that the client reviews for final approval.

On a months- or years-long project, the stage version will likely be shown to the client at regular intervals so they can review features iteratively. For example, at the end of the first month, you might review features one through three; at the end of the second month, you might review features four through six. Alternatively, the client may review a clickable prototype (a first representation of an end product) followed by iterations of increasingly functional versions of the product. However they're done, these iterative reviews focus everyone's attention on a manageable set of features and minimize the chances of too many changes coming in at the very end.

Transition from development to stage

To create the stage version, the team (usually the developers) deploys the development version to an environment that either will become, or is identical to, the final environment. In the case of a web-based site or application, this means a server. For a mobile app, this means a stage version of the app that can be manually installed on different devices for review.

The stage version should be isolated from any programming changes; all new work and any changes to existing work are done on the development version and then pushed out on a schedule, thereby keeping the stage version stable.

Review the stage version internally

Once the stage version is up and running, have the internal team do a thorough review. A lot can change between the early days of the project and the stage version. You want to be sure that contributors agree that their work was incorporated and interpreted correctly in the end product before quality assurance (QA) begins.

This is especially important for the front-end track. Start with a meeting between user experience architecture (UXA), design, and front-end development to review everything together. While this won't be the first time they're talking about and looking over the work they produce, it's a formal checkpoint.

Ensure that the front-end developer has reviewed their work in a variety of browsers (not full-on testing, but at least a review to ensure that no major issues exist). Ask the developers to give their work a quick once-over as well.

Complete all internal review prior to quality assurance (QA). If testers find major gaffes that the team should have noticed earlier, it wastes time. Because when things change, retesting is required. And when that happens too often, it's not efficient, cheap, or fun.

Final Content

aka The Story

Final content is the copy, imagery, and every other piece of content that will be published in the launch version of the end product.

OWNER:

CONTENT STRATEGIST

CONTRIBUTORS:

PROJECT MANAGER   CLIENT   DESIGNER

DESCRIPTION:

Final content is all the images, words, videos, etc. that are in place when the live product goes public at launch time. It's been planned for and developed over the course of the production phase and is added to the stage version of the product for review.

"Final" is a bit misleading, since many projects require changes and updates after launch. In this case, final refers to publish-ready content that populates the product when it launches.

SPECIAL CONSIDERATIONS:

- Outline all content needs early so there is no unexpected content to create.

- As content is developed, review against the messaging and tone agreed to in the strategy and user experience brief.

- All content should work at the service of a stated project goal.

- A copywriter may also be involved in this deliverable.

LOCATION IN THE PROCESS:

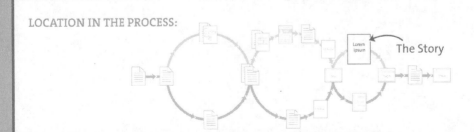

The Story

Finalize content for launch

Content never stops. Here, "final" content just means that it's ready to go live.

Over the course of the project, the client and the content strategist should have developed a plan for creating final launch content (Cheat Sheet 013). Together, they determined what was needed, how it would get done, and who would do it. If that isn't the case, go directly to Jail; do not pass GO. (Or at least return to Chapters 7 and 8 and read up on the importance of planning for content.)

Now, it's time for the project manager to step in and make a plan to add content to the stage version.

The goal is to have as much final launch content in place as possible when the client reviews the stage version. The more realistic the stage version is, the better. If it doesn't feel real, the client and the internal team can more easily brush off details with the rationale, "it will be updated later." You don't want this. This is how "Copy goes here" or "Lorem Ipsum" ends up on a live site.

> **YEAH, BUT…** Isn't "Lorem Ipsum" copy better than nothing?

> **GLAD YOU ASKED…** Maybe. But, what's worse? Going live with a blank spot on the site, or going live with placeholder copy tucked away on an internal page. It's sometimes easier to "see" a blank space than it is to see something that looks almost right. But the important thing is to make sure it's someone's job to check that all content was created, and that it's in its proper place in the product.

There are two general scenarios for content: content that will remain largely the same after launch, and content that will need ongoing updates. The path to the stage version and client review varies slightly depending on which type of content you're dealing with.

Manage for (relatively) static content

It's rare for websites these days, but mobile apps, digital installations, and kiosks are examples of products that often have relatively static content. If they have changes, they're done less regularly than on a website. In these cases, content should be delivered over the course of the production stage. The content strategist, project manager, and client should be working collaboratively to make sure there's not a frantic push for content or massive, last-minute changes to the direction or substance of the content.

This milestone is about checking off the content you have against the original requirements, doing a final assessment and read-through, and getting any approvals you need. If you've planned well, there should be no surprises.

YEAH BUT…What if the content is too long? Or too short?

GLAD YOU ASKED…That's what the stage version review is for. It allows the team to see the content in place so it can be evaluated in the end product environment. Content often looks different in the "real" setting, so be prepared to review carefully and critically!

Manage for dynamic content

Many websites require the client to regularly update certain pages or sections. In these cases, the correlation between final launch content and stage version is less linear. There are two routes you can take to get content placed: share the workload with the client, or do it internally.

In a perfect world you'd split the task of populating the stage version with final launch content between the internal team and the client. First, have the internal team get some of the content into place to illustrate what it should look like and how it works. Then use part of stage version review (coming up shortly) to show the client how to add and change content. Think of it like a practice run at how they'll use the product in the real world.

In the real world, projects are often hurtling toward launch day without enough time to split the content task with the client. It's often much faster for the internal team to take care of it and train the client later on how to use and manage the site.

However it gets done, it's imperative that final launch content is ready and in place for review in the stage version.

Project manager checkpoint

As the finishing touches are made, the project manager watches for any details that may derail a project at the last minute. He monitors reviews and approvals to ensure that the right people are seeing what they need to see, documents any new developments, watches for changes in one area that may affect other departments, and observes expertise areas to confirm information is flowing freely. Even a small blockage in communication at this stage of the project can affect the deadline. It's the project manager's job to avoid this.

Verify the work

Quality assurance is a bridge between the end user and the team that creates the product. They're the first line of offense for the user, and the last line of defense for the internal team. This stage ensures that the end user is going to get the experience he expects and makes sure that your you-know-what is covered.

Have realistic expectations

Technology creates tension. This is a point we brought up in Chapter 4, "Communication," when we discussed prepping the client for the project. At the test stage, it's worth making two points about realistic expectations: technology is always evolving and products must be optimized.

It's beneficial to communicate these truths to the client and to explain that testing—now and in the future—ensures that the project is set up to succeed within these parameters.

Technology evolves

Every product is built at a particular moment in time within the available range of technology. As software is updated, as programs disappear, and as new devices are developed, your client's product will have to change, too. This is how technology works: it's evolutionary. Successful testing now won't guarantee that the product will perform as successfully in six months. Communicate to clients that testing is necessary but results are specific to that time and technology.

FACT: Testing is not a guarantee

The need for, and purpose of, quality assurance (QA) in digital projects is different than in other media. Once you approve a TV spot or proofread a print ad, it never changes. And it'll look the same on everyone's TV or in their magazine. The same is not true of digital products. There are many factors (connection speed, hardware, browser, plug-ins, user goals) that affect how—and how well—an end user will interact with a product. Many of these things are out of the team's and the client's control. QA gives everyone the confidence that the product will work in *most* cases. But, there's no guarantee that it will work in all cases. And, if it doesn't work, there's no guarantee that it was the fault of the product.

THINK ABOUT: **Edge cases**

You can't design for every case, but you should think about them all. Consider how to make the end product *the best it can be* outside the scope of the target audience and prioritized devices. We call this *degrading gracefully*. Think about how features will work and how design will look as the end product is used in these edge cases. For example, if a user doesn't have a required plug-in, what will the site look like? While it can't be perfect for everyone, aim to make it functional for as many users as possible.

Products must be optimized

Accepting that products can't be all things to all people opens the door to the most effective thinking about how to make it the best thing for the people that matter most. The team made decisions that optimized the end product for a specific target audience. Certain browsers and devices were prioritized over others, which in turn means that the product may be barely usable in certain low-priority environments. That's how it *has* to be. Testing helps your team and the client understand how the product will perform in the low-priority environments, but may not fix it.

Test the end product

ASSIGN TESTING

If you don't have a quality assurance department, assign someone to be the tester for your project. While it's ideal to have a trained team, it's also invaluable to have an individual who didn't produce the work review everything. He'll have a more objective eye and a fresh perspective.

Testing is how the internal team makes sure the product that's delivered matches what was promised in the beginning.

Testers break things, find holes, discover vulnerabilities, question choices, and challenge infrastructure. It's their job to stir the pot, to create a little conflict, and to ask team members to explain their work. They're the interactive industry's equivalent of editors and proofreaders; developers can't test their own code just as writers can't proof their own writing.

There's no such thing as bug-free code. Period. Testers can test until money runs out and there will still be bugs. Communicating this to your client early on will help establish realistic expectations about the product. But be careful how you explain it. It's not that testing is futile. The promise of testing is to ensure some level of quality with regard to what is released. The team and the client agree on what that level of quality is (based on risk, budget, and timeline), and they test to that level. If other bugs are discovered later, the team either fixes them as part of the original agreement or as part of a maintenance plan. The key is to help clients and stakeholders understand that testing is an essential part of the process, but it doesn't guarantee perfection.

What are we testing for?

Testers check end products on many levels. Beyond making sure links work and images load, they ensure that things work as they're supposed to: the UXA, design, development, interfaces, data flow, security, and functionality. They're determining the quality level of the entire product.

USER EXPERIENCE DESIGN. Testers assess two things when it comes to user experience: how well the product works when it's used as expected, and whether the end product meets the goals and strategies as outlined in the project documentation.

PRODUCT DURABILITY. Testers try to disprove what the requirements definition (RD) says. If the RD says a feature is supposed to work one way, the testers do anything they can to *not* make it work that way. Like, what happens if a form field is filled out incorrectly, or not at all? Testers try to find holes in every part of the product.

SECURITY. Testers confirm that expectations about security meet the requirements established in the RD. They ensure that security measures work as they should and that those security measures are the right ones for the product.

The level of security and the corresponding level of testing depend on the nature of the product. If a website is collecting credit card information, it has to be PCI-DSS compliant—and testing is required to verify that compliance. If there's potential monetary benefit for the user (as in loyalty programs or online contests), testing rigorously verifies registration conditions and looks for loopholes that can be exploited. At all levels of security, think of how to protect the clients' and users' information and interests.

TESTERS AND CUSTOMER SUPPORT

Testers can learn a lot about general user patterns by tracking customer support and service calls. By observing customer frustrations and questions about all products, they can help prevent common misunderstandings in future projects.

SELLING QA

If there's no budget in your projects for quality assurance (QA), you might find yourself having to convince others that it's important. Phrase it like this: Testing mitigates risk, for both your team and the client. Thorough testing can prevent embarrassing blunders.

TIP: **Error messages show how much you care**

A user is likely to be frustrated when he comes across an error message. He's trying to do something but can't. This is a critical user experience moment. Think of error messages as a lifeline to someone in trouble, not a slap on the hand to someone who's been bad. Route unsupportive or unclear messages back through the team to get them rewritten.

Push to get the best

QA questions decisions. Sometimes this can challenge the ego of whoever did the original work. The project manager should allow and encourage this kind of agitation. If you have a culture that's truly collaborative, team members should welcome challenges and criticism because it leads to a better end product. As the project manager, make sure the team understands that the role of testers is to ask questions.

Testers are invaluable throughout the entire project. For best results, they should be involved from the very beginning. As the RD is being written, testers offer a unique perspective on features and functionality. While developers are thinking about how to make things work, testers are thinking about all the ways in which those same things *won't* work. Sounds a bit contrary, right? It is, and that's exactly why it's an asset.

Draft a test plan

The test plan is the document that QA uses to itemize the things they're verifying (Cheat Sheet 014).

The test plan gets *used* here, but it's been a work-in-progress since the development approach was approved (see Chapter 8, "Project Production"). Writing the test plan is a testing process in itself: it's testing the RD. As testers compose the test plan, they'll ask questions about conditions and requirements that help the developers shape their own work.

Where the RD lists everything that the developers expect to happen, the test plan asks, "What happens if…?" over and over again for each feature.

QUALITY
ASSURANCE

Test Plan

aka The Bouncer

The test plan verifies that features and functionality meet developer, client, and end-user expectations.

OWNER:

TESTER

CONTRIBUTORS:

PRODUCTION
LEAD

BACK-END
DEVELOPER

TECH LEAD

DESCRIPTION:

Test plans verify that approved functionality, user experience architecture, and design satisfy stakeholder expectations. Testers verify that features behave as expected, and that any unintended actions are handled in a graceful manner.

The test plan merges information from project documentation to translate features into a combination of scenarios (test cases) and anticipated behaviors (expected results). Additionally, testers explore the behavior of unintended functionality; "What happens if..." is a charter for exploratory testing.

When testers find errors or inconsistencies, they create bug reports that communicate issues to developers. Writing a complete and thorough bug report is critical to timely and effective fixes.

SPECIAL CONSIDERATIONS:

- Test plans are a preventative document. Test plans can identify holes in the requirements definition and information architecture. Testers should review those documents to save time and money before testing even begins.

- As the project evolves, so does the test plan. Test cases must be added or adjusted to accommodate all changes.

LOCATION IN THE PROCESS:

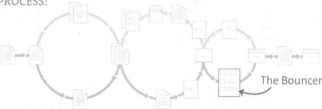

The Bouncer

Test cases and bug reports

To create a test plan, the team writes **test cases**. While executing a test plan, the team writes **bug reports**.

TEST TEMPLATE

Write standard test cases for conditions and features that your team routinely checks. This minimizes duplicative work and ensures consistency and accuracy.

Test cases outline specific operations that need to be verified during QA. These test cases provide a framework for checking the features and functionality. Although this framework isn't an exhaustive checklist (there are many more little details that all testers will check along the way), it's a great guide and artifact for the team.

As features and functionality are tested, bugs will arise. Effectively communicating the conditions around each bug is as important as finding them. Developers rely on bug reports to make the repairs.

When testers alert developers about bugs, developers react one of two ways: agree that it's indeed a bug and fix it or disagree because the feature works—for better or worse—as it was requested.

If the feature meets technical requirements, the issue usually comes down to whether it meets user expectations. Testers may keep the "bug" flagged if they believe that the end user will experience the feature as a problem. At this point the resolution will require conversation with the team to determine what, if anything, will be changed.

THINK ABOUT: The mighty bug

A well-written bug report identifies a defect and clearly describes the steps required to reproduce the problem. Bugs allow a team to quickly triage defects and focus their efforts on the most critical or effective changes required before releasing a product. A bug report provides a place for documented discussion and communication of corrections. Once corrected, a bug should be verified by the QA team and closed. Testing and refactoring is a critical part of creating a safe and reliable product and bugs provide the reports and communication network for these changes.

Project manager checkpoint

Testing can cause friction within your team. Testers are critically reviewing work that, at times, will need to be fixed. As the project manager, it's crucial that you monitor the discussions and communication among team members to keep it productive and on track. (See Chapter 4, "Communication," for ideas on managing conflict.)

The main focus for the project manager during testing is ensuring that bugs are getting resolved. Watch for arguments between testers and the team about whether or not certain bugs are actually bugs ("That's not a bug, it's a feature!") and for bugs that trigger possible changes to the product (scope alert!).

Stage: The dress rehearsal

The stage version is a fully functional version of the end product that the client tests and reviews (Cheat Sheet 015). It's the client's opportunity to evaluate the end product based on their expectations, in a process called user acceptance testing (in this case "user" refers to the client, not the end user).

Present the stage version

For the client, and for the team, this is an important moment. Treat it with care and really think about how to present the product to the client.

Consider Tiffany's. (Yes, *that* Tiffany's.) Sure, they have nice jewelry, but a big part of the experience is that signature blue box with the white ribbon. Think about how to make the presentation of the stage version a "blue box" moment. Doing so acknowledges the hard work of the team and the investment of the client.

WHO FROM THE CLIENT SIDE SHOULD BE AT THE PRESENTATION? Sometimes the main project contact, or a small subset of the client group, will want to review the stage version before it goes to the wider client team. Talk to your main client contact about the order of events and reviews: who should be there, and how many presentations should happen.

Stage Version
aka The Sneak Peek

The stage version is a review-ready product that looks and works like the final end product.

OWNERS:

FRONT-END DEVELOPER   BACK-END DEVELOPER

CONTRIBUTORS:

PROJECT   TECH LEAD   PRODUCTION   TESTER
MANAGER   LEAD

CREATIVE LEAD   DESIGNER   RELATIONSHIP
                        MANAGER

DESCRIPTION:

A stage version is the closest thing to the end product that the client and internal team will see prior to launch. Complete back-end and front-end programming is deployed from the development version to the stage version. To this, copy and assets are added.

The stage version is like a dress rehearsal for the end product. The stage version allows the client to see nearly-complete elements of the end product. It may be an almost whole product, while other times it will be distinct pieces. Either way, what you show the client should be functionally stable and visually accurate.

SPECIAL CONSIDERATIONS:

• The staging server environment should be identical to the live version to confirm that all functionality will work as expected.

• Changes are never done on the stage version, they're always done on the development version.

• If the client will be entering content, the stage version can be a good place for training and data entry.

LOCATION IN THE PROCESS:

The Sneak Peek

WHO FROM YOUR TEAM SHOULD BE THERE? Sometimes it's good to include specific internal team members who can explain technical information to the client, like the developer or tester. If the client is more concerned about user experience, perhaps a designer or user experience architect would be a better fit. Use your knowledge of the client's needs to think about the people on your team who would foster the best experience.

HOW SHOULD IT BE PRESENTED? If a meeting is possible, do it. In a meeting, you can control how the stage version is unveiled, and it's easier to read the clients' faces for nonverbal reactions. It's also a much easier way to gather initial feedback and answer any questions. A conference call (or webcast) can be an effective second choice if a meeting isn't possible. And if you *must* send the information electronically, include your "presentation" in the body of the email.

Explain the review process

Outline what will happen during the review process, what the client's role will be, and how your team will respond. Set expectations and establish a plan from the start.

Walk through the product

Give the client a formal tour of the new product. Explain the functionality, the features, and how it works as a whole. Point out features that you know are important to them; show off features that the team is proud of, or that are expected to be important for end users.

If the client will be managing content or updates, be clear about what exactly they'll need to do and where to do it. This isn't the time for extensive training, but you want them to know which specific features they'll be using day in, day out. Making sure those elements match up exactly with what they want increases the chance that they'll successfully and seamlessly use the end product once it's live.

Give direction

This may be the first time your client has reviewed a website, app, or whatever it is you've built for them. Make sure they put on their critical thinking caps and realize the importance of this stage. This is the dress rehearsal: things should be near perfect.

Explain that they should:

REVIEW DOCUMENTS. Tell the client which project documents to use as reference points (hint: the RD and the strategy and UX brief). Using these as guides helps keep reviews focused and structured. Walk through a feature as it's written in the RD and then explain how to use that description to evaluate the feature in real life.

SEND SAMPLE FEEDBACK

Create a few samples of good feedback. Make one an example of subjective feedback ("we're not liking the link color") and another an example of functional feedback ("the form doesn't respond correctly when I don't use a prefix"). Show the client how to explain subjective points and how to give evidence with technological points.

THINK LIKE A USER. At this point, it's easy for some to slide into what "I" don't like. Keep energy and attention on the business goals. They should keep asking the question, "If I were a user, what would I want to do? What do I need to achieve?"

EVALUATE BUSINESS-SIDE OPERATIONS. Throughout development, the internal team has worked closely with any required software or third-party vendors on the client side. Now, have the client test how well the product integrates with the operational systems they have in place. To test integration, collaboratively develop a plan for how to accurately assess the performance and effectiveness of these infrastructure details.

MAKE FEEDBACK EFFECTIVE. Constructing a good bug report isn't instinctive. Give your client the right checklist for creating thorough, useful reports: type of device, browser (if it's a browser-based product), and steps outlining the exact actions that led to the error. Explain that to fix it the developers have to replicate the problem and isolate the cause.

Keep subjective feedback separate from bug reports; they have very different content and frequently result in different conversations and solutions. Keeping them separate will enable better communication and allow you to get the right information to the right people with greater ease.

Create a communication plan

At the feedback stage, having one point of contact on the client side is indispensible. Your sanity will thank you later.

From the outset of the stage version review process, determine two things: who on the client side will be communicating feedback, and how it will be communicated. Have as few people as possible (one is ideal) corresponding from the client side, and use a single document to capture the feedback. If the client has several distinct departments reviewing the product, one contact per department is just as helpful. Narrowing communication to a primary person is important for two reasons:

SILENCE ISN'T GOLDEN

If the client says, "We love it" and gives no further feedback, be wary. It's great that they love it, but no feedback usually means that they didn't really dig in. Ask them pointed questions about features and design elements to get them thinking critically.

PRIORITIZING. Does it matter that Joe in Human Resources doesn't like the layout of the product page? The client contact should separate the feedback that matters from the stuff that doesn't.

ORGANIZING. Client-organized feedback allows the project manager to focus on distributing work and prioritizing tasks on your side. Furthermore, it prevents the project manager from getting the same bug report three times.

The open and honest relationship you've developed with the client has immense benefits at this late stage. If they request a major change that would derail the launch date, talk openly with them about the realities of implementing the changes. Talk about the actual value of the change and the costs of the changes (not just financial costs, but time and energy). Be direct about the realities and be collaborative about finding a good solution.

FACT: Fixing bugs = more testing

Fixing bugs requires new code. Adding new code means that existing code might be affected. That in turn necessitates more testing. This cycle of testing, fixing, testing can feel long, and perhaps redundant, for team members not familiar with it. Proactively explain this part of the process so impatience doesn't set in.

Bug tracking

Bug tracking can be done in a variety of ways, but no matter how you handle it, make sure it accommodates separate internal and client tracking.

Keeping the internal and client comments separate means that you don't have to translate points unnecessarily. Internal teams and clients speak different languages (more on that later). This language barrier means that you don't want them seeing each other's feedback. Internal teams use direct language that isn't always client-friendly; client feedback will probably need refining before it is passed on to developers. Keeping the documents separate allows the right energy to be spent on the right task.

Support your team

While you're encouraging the client to critically and thoroughly review the end product and voice their feedback, hearing all of it may be deflating for your team. Remind them that just because there is a lot of assessing, conversing, and tweaking, they didn't drop the ball on anything. This is part of the process.

Think about ways to channel feedback so the team understands the client's intention and the concern, not only the criticism.

Accurate project documentation is invaluable during the review process. As questions are coming in, it's crucial that you be able to trace your footsteps back to the reason why every decision was made. Having a point of reference for exactly why a feature works the way it does or why a link goes to what it does can make the review process smoother, more diplomatic, and less subjective.

Set priorities for the client and your team

During crunch periods, make sure that priorities and "need to have" elements are accomplished before "nice to have" ones.

EXPLAIN TESTING TIME TO CLIENTS. As they're reviewing and finding things they want to tweak, the client might feel like turnaround time on the changes is too long. They're probably not trying to be difficult; many just don't have a realistic sense of how long things take. Explain that a small change to code in one place means retesting throughout the section.

ENSURE THAT THE TEST TEAM IS FOCUSED ON PRIORITIES. QA teams are thorough, critical, and can often be perfectionist by nature. That's why they're so good at their jobs. Be sure to balance priorities, time, and budget. Don't let perfect be the enemy of launch.

Realize that team members speak different languages

Clients and testers don't use the same words when they talk about problems.

DON'T SHOW CLIENTS INTERNAL RESPONSES TO FEEDBACK WITHOUT REVIEWING IT. Most testers and developers will respond to feedback in terms the client won't entirely understand. They're focused on getting the problem fixed, not communicating diplomatically and clearly to the client. For example, a valid developer response to a bug report is "won't fix"; taken verbatim that can seem pretty blunt and uncooperative to a client. (And that's why they usually shouldn't have access to the internal teams' bug tracking documentation.) That's where the project manager must be translating industry-speak into whatever language makes sense to the client. "Won't fix" in developer terms can translate to something like this to a client: "This isn't a valid bug because it aligns with what was written in the RD. Should we let this go for now, or consider a change to this feature before we launch?" Big difference.

REVIEW AND CLARIFY FEEDBACK FROM CLIENTS. Most clients are unaccustomed to communicating problems in ways that satisfy testers' highly structured way of approaching bugs. To a client, "This doesn't work" can seem like an appropriate report, but it will drive testers crazy. Make sure all the necessary information is included in the feedback—even if that means a lot of back and forth with the client—because without all the critical pieces of information, the feedback isn't helpful.

Project manager checkpoint

As the client reviews the end product, difficult moments may arise between your team and the client or even among your internal team itself. As the launch date looms, keeping communication effective is as critical as ever. The project manager is performing two hugely important tasks during the peak review stage: liaising and translating.

As discussions and debates come up, it's useful to externalize the conversation. Emphasize that it's always about the end product and the end users. That's the mantra the *entire* team needs to repeat over and over.

When disputes come up, and they will, always go back to the documentation that guided the project. Every single deliverable was created for a reason— to provide specific guidance and to capture specific information. The value of project documentation is both as a guide while creating the product, and as a reference when reviewing the product.

Takeaways

Staging brings an unusual set of factors to the project: tasks have slowed down and the number of active team members has diminished, but emotions and pressure run higher. It's great to have emotional energy on a project, but like all things human, it's always more productive if it's managed appropriately.

Throughout this stage, your team put the final touches on the stage version and then tested it, inside and out. Everyone had their critical thinking caps on to ensure that every detail is done as perfectly as possible.

Once the client approves the stage version, it's gonna go live.

10

PROJECT LAUNCH

Hello, world

Launching the product is what you've been waiting for. The energy, planning, thinking, and executing have been leading up to this culminating moment. After your team takes care of a few remaining details, you're ready to launch.

In this chapter, we'll discuss

- Handoff: Passing the client the baton
- Last call: Team review and approval
- Launch: 3, 2, 1…Blastoff

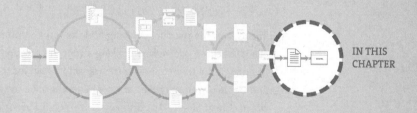

IN THIS
CHAPTER

Whether it's a three-week project or a two-year project, the team has invested time, energy, and hard work into bringing the goals and technology together to create a successful digital solution. The emotions and pressure that built up throughout the project are at an all-time high as launch day approaches.

Passing the client the baton

Unlike traditional media, interactive projects produce *living* products. Post-launch, they require work—sometimes more work than it took to create them.

Even short-lived products, like promotions or contests, require some action on the part of the team or client (if only to monitor for fraud). And relatively static products like an app require monitoring of reviews and crash reports, and pushing out updates. Giving the client the right tools and information at this stage is key to seeing them—and the project—succeed. If they fail to understand the evolutionary, living nature of the product and their role in its lifespan, then the project won't be truly effective.

Exactly what you deliver and what you do at this stage will vary depending on the client and the project. Give your client tools and training that empower them to manage the product.

Launch is just the beginning

Between the moment of the client's approval of the stage version and the launch of the live version, teach the client how to use the finalized end product. Equipping the client to maintain and update the product after launch is critical to a successful project. Launch isn't the end, it's the beginning.

The idea of the product evolving and the task of updating won't be new to the client (because you've been talking about this throughout the project, right?), but now is the time to initiate the transition. Plan for training in the timeline and begin developing the support materials once the final features are nailed down (Cheat Sheet 016). Training isn't a roadblock or hurdle on the way to launch; it's there to ensure post-launch success.

CHEAT SHEET 016

Support Materials
aka The Safety Net

Support materials are the assorted reference materials created to successfully pass ownership of the end product to the client.

OWNER:

PROJECT MANAGER

CONTRIBUTORS:

CONTENT STRATEGIST

TECH LEAD

CREATIVE LEAD

DESIGNER

FRONT-END DEVELOPER

ACCOUNT STRATEGIST

RELATIONSHIP MANAGER

DESCRIPTION:

Training or reference materials help clients become familiar with and effectively use the end product. They enable clients to be active and independent owners of their website or application.

Materials will vary for each project but common ones are training and product manuals, support information, and content and style guides. The goal is to give the people operating the product the tools they need to feel comfortable and empowered.

SPECIAL CONSIDERATIONS:

- While training the client, listen for repeated questions or details that appear more difficult to grasp, and include helpful information about those details in the support materials.

- Ask the client what information they would like to have easily available, and provide it.

LOCATION IN THE PROCESS:

The Safety Net

Prepare for future content

During both planning and production, the content strategists (either on the team, on the client side, or both) put together final launch content and wrote content plans to keep the product updated and on-message into the future.

Deliverables typically include things like a style guide, a workflow plan, and an editorial calendar. These tools enable the client to prepare content, determine governance, and execute effectively.

If your internal team is providing any of these deliverables, the content strategist, creative lead, and client should work together over the course of the project to make them as thorough and realistic as possible. Each document will evolve as the project is refined and should reflect the design, strategy, and functionality of the final product.

TRAIN BEFORE LAUNCH

Always train in advance of the launch date, and develop your training plan even earlier. Outline what features will need explanation and make a plan that ensures that happens.

Train the client

The client must be comfortable and in control of this new thing they have. If they will be managing content, schedule official training sessions.

Start with frequent users, who will likely need to know the product on a far more detailed level than others. Their training should be as thorough as you can get without their eyes glazing over. Once you get them on board with how everything works, they can assist other users as they learn.

Don't underestimate your clients. Clients are empowered when they know more than just what they "need" to know. Quick and easy editing tools are great, but they're even better when the user understands what the tools are doing. Consider, for example, making edits using basic HTML versus using a web editor. Why only teach a tool that obfuscates what's happening under the hood when you can teach what's actually happening? Frequently, this gives the client a broader understanding to use the tools more effectively and troubleshoot problems that may come up.

Produce and distribute a product manual

Any technical information that helps the client operate the product should be gathered into a product or reference manual. This should serve as a standalone reference and potentially as a starter training kit for future users. Often there are two resources: the overall product manual and instructions specific to the project.

Outline a support plan

Many large projects require ongoing customer support to help the client make easy transitions as technology evolves, and as new employees are hired and features are updated. Outline the information your client will need if they have post-launch support questions. If you're in an agency, check with the account team to see if and how this was planned for in the budget. If nothing was planned at the outset of the project, work with the client to develop a plan now. You don't want the support information to be a surprise, especially since it's supposed to be just that: supportive.

The client should know

- Who to contact if there's a technical problem

- Who to contact for additional training or product maintenance

- If it's a website, where it's hosted, whether the site needs monitoring (and who will do this if it does), and what the escalation plan is in the event of downtime

There might be more that you hand off to a client, or there might be less. The materials you provide don't have to answer every potential question, but they should be thorough enough so the client knows where and how to find answers or help.

Project manager checkpoint

As launch approaches and the team is gathering support materials for post-launch, make sure that the client feels comfortable with owning and managing the end product. This will mean different things for every client and every project. Use the open communication channels you've created with the client to discuss what they need and want. In all cases, think about—and ask!—what the client needs to be an effective owner.

The final green light

After the client approves the stage version, there's one final review and approval process for the internal team to go through. This represents the last call for small tweaks, like shifting a line or adjusting a graphic.

Review the final version

Team members should do the final review from two perspectives. First, does this launch-day version of the site align with the goals and strategies outlined in the strategy and user experience brief? Secondly, does it meet the quality standard of both the company and the individual team member?

If you've effectively used the brief and department review meetings throughout the project, these questions should yield no objections, and if they do, the concerns should be minor. If objections are raised that *do* question the effectiveness or quality of the product, you have a problem. D'oh! That's a challenge this late in the game, but it can happen. Mitigate this potentially high-pressure situation with a little thoughtfulness and transparency.

ASSESS. Determine whether the client needs to be a part of the solution. If your team messed up—hey, it happens!—it might be that the client doesn't have to do anything to correct course. These are things that just need to be corrected—and fast. And the client is none the wiser. On the other hand, there will be times when the problem is the result of an oversight by the team and the client, and reaching a good solution will require the client's participation.

MEASURE. Assess the impact of dealing with the problem from budgetary, timing, and personnel perspectives.

COMMUNICATE. If need be, present the problem to the client. If the problem requires no work on their part but will affect the timeline, explain the plan to fix the problem. If you have to collaborate with them to reach a solution, outline the best way to do that. Always go into the conversation with at least one possible solution and outline what you know and propose to do. The discussion should be as goal-oriented and solution-focused as possible.

At times, the internal team will determine that a change requiring a lot of time or resources must be done in order to make the project successful. If this happens, leadership should step in and work with the client. It demonstrates that you support the proposed solution, that you recognize the importance of the issue, and that you value the client's business. It's going to be hard—delivering bad news always is—but if you've developed a good relationship with them you can tackle the solution collaboratively. It's glamorous at the top.

Approve the final version

Obtaining a thumbs-up from the entire internal team is a critical people moment. It's important to continue the buy-in message to the very end. The team should have as much investment in the last moments of the project as in the first moments. Moreover, asking each team member to give his personal thumbs-up before the product goes live encourages him to actually agree with the way it turned out. And buy-in plus agreement equals an empowered team.

These approvals can be gathered in any number of ways, from a casual, verbal approval to a formal signature on a launch approval form. Do what seems best for your team and your company culture—the important thing is the act of asking for a final thumbs-up from the people who built the product.

CONSCIENTIOUS OBJECTORS

If you ask for agreement, there's a chance you won't get it entirely. Allow people to voice their concerns. The answer might be, "Thanks, we'll fix that before we launch," or it might be "Sorry, but we're launching anyway," but at least they had a chance to be heard.

THINK ABOUT: URLs as a business asset

Working on a website redesign? Make sure that all old URLs *permanently* redirect to the new URLs. Existing URLs have acquired value with search engines over time. If you don't redirect these old URLs to the new ones, the redesigned site won't inherit any of the previous site's rankings with search engines. And that can be a massive loss for the client.

Project manager checkpoint

As you move through final approvals, your primary task is communicating with the team. These last few tasks of reviewing and approving sound simple, but at times, there is a lot of work happening in the days leading right up to launch. When this is the case, there's a good deal of cross-disciplinary communication and task tracking. As tweaks are made, testing may have to jump in and reexamine certain details, and the project manager should be obsessively monitoring any changes to ensure that all possible consequences are considered.

Flipping the switch

This is it: The product's going live! At this point the stage version is moved to the live servers and the product is ready for users.

Technical expertise and precision are vitally important at this moment. There are many details to consider and check off as you approach the actual launch moment and as your team moves past it.

Launch on a Wednesday after lunch

When you launch a website, there are a few good times, and there are many horrible times, to do it. Here's a handy rule: Launch on Wednesday, right after lunch. Why?

PEAK PERFORMANCE. Your team is warmed up by mid-week. With Monday and Tuesday under their belts, they've taken care of any on-fire emails that came in over the weekend. After lunch means that their stomachs are full and their minds are alert. These are perfect conditions.

AVAILABILITY. You don't want your team to have to stay late into the night or extend themselves over the weekend to responsibly manage a launch. Late hours and weekends happen, but you shouldn't make a plan that necessitates them. Furthermore, other companies aren't open on weekends so if you have partnerships or if you're using any third-party products, you won't have the support system *you* need to provide effective support for your client.

MONITORING. Once a site launches, it's critical to see how it performs and to be able to make changes in real time. There are always adjustments after launch because new conditions can affect technology. You need everyone on high alert for two to three days after you go live. It isn't ideal to wait for a weekend to go by before making a change or fixing a problem. Moreover, as the team is monitoring, questions for the client might come up, and, guess what? They're probably not working over the weekend, either.

If you can't make Wednesday work, Tuesdays and Thursdays are decent alternatives. But avoid Mondays and Fridays whenever possible. And run screaming from launches on January 1.

> When creating a timeline, think critically, carefully, and early about the launch date. Work closely with your client to find an optimal time. If it's a less-than-ideal day, make as many plans as you can to get it as close to ideal as you can.

A few weeks before launch

Gather all launch considerations into one master list. Make a checklist of everything you have to do or think about, and then share it with the team. All minds should be on the critical details so nothing dumb gets overlooked.

Determine external requirements

Contact the hosting service to get a checklist of everything *they* need to ensure a smooth launch. (We host most of the websites we make at Clockwork, so we coordinate with our in-house system administrators.) If you're working with an external hosting company, find a dedicated service representative who will help you through the launch. If, on the other hand, your client is self-hosting, be in direct contact with their IT department. As with an external hosting company, find a single point of contact on the IT staff to work with. Exact needs may vary between project and department, but the important thing is to know exact launch requirements way before launch.

Outline internal requirements

Have a standard list of things to check when it comes to projects. Start making it project-specific several weeks before launch. This can be anything from networking logistics to which room at the office you're going to use as a command center. The project manager should work closely with the tech lead and the system administrators (in-house or external) to make sure all considerations are outlined for the team and client.

Master checklists are incredibly helpful in high-energy and high-stress situations. Checklists bring order to chaos and allow minds to focus on managing what's happening rather than what to remember. The beauty of a generic list is that it can be easily customized for each project, dropping tasks that are unnecessary and assigning remaining tasks to specific team members.

For websites, standard tasks may include

- Configuring domain name service (DNS)

- Purchasing security certificates

- Installing security certificates

Combine your internal requirements list with the external requirements. Listing these together in a master version minimizes the chance that something will be forgotten and gets people and timing organized around critical tasks.

Estimate lag time

One important detail that clients rarely think about is the lag time between the moment the product goes live and when the site or app becomes widely available. Prep them for this lag so they aren't disappointed or feel like something went wrong.

LIST EVERYTHING

Does it seem redundant to have "purchase" and "install" security certificates on the final launch checklist? It's not. Be detailed and specific. There's a lot going on, so it's best to include every important task. Plus, different team members might execute the related tasks so this allows you to assign and track them accordingly.

LEARN MORE: Recommended reading

If you want to know about the wonders of checklists, why they're so useful, and how to make them effective, read *The Checklist Manifesto: How to Get Things Right* by Atul Gawande.[1]

---

1 Metropolitan Books, 2009

Live Version

aka The Real Deal

This is it: the end product.

OWNER:

CLIENT

CONTRIBUTORS:

SYSTEM
ADMINISTRATOR

USER EXPERIENCE
ARCHITECT

CREATIVE LEAD

DESIGNER

PRODUCTION
LEAD

TECH LEAD

TESTER

PROJECT
MANAGER

ACCOUNT
STRATEGIST

RELATIONSHIP
MANAGER

FRONT-END
DEVELOPER

DESCRIPTION:

The live version is the end product that is publicly available. It contains fully tested content, code, and functionality.

Once the stage version is approved, the product goes live. The transition from stage to live is the product launch. After launch, all content and functionality must be reviewed to ensure that it still looks and works as expected.

SPECIAL CONSIDERATIONS:

- Like the stage version, development work should never be done on the live version.

- If metric capturing is enabled, take steps to ensure that internal testing activity is not recorded as legitimate visitor traffic.

- All live websites should be monitored by a system administrator for availability and response time.

LOCATION IN THE PROCESS:

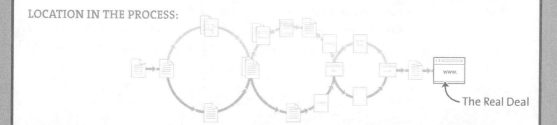

The Real Deal

If your client must have something up and available to users by a certain day and time, be sure to determine the lag time very early on. (For a website, this lag is "time to live" or TTL. For an iOS app, it's the time it takes for Apple to approve it for the iTunes store.) Also, pad your timeline a little in case something goes wrong or it simply takes longer than you expected.

Create a launch day plan

As conditions change, technology reacts. This means that issues may arise when transitioning from the stage version to the live version (Cheat Sheet 017). Your team is migrating an entire website or app to a real host site and going live, which changes the conditions under which it's operating.

You can't anticipate everything that may come up, but if you've prepared for what will definitely happen you'll have more energy to focus on any unexpected things that arise.

CREATE A COMMAND CENTER. If you're launching a large website, convene your internal team in a command room to monitor the launch. Have the client (or at least a representative) on the phone or readily available. Together, review the site as it goes live. Prepare the team to spend about two to four hours monitoring, or however long it takes to thoroughly go through all the features and the full scope of content.

RETESTING CHECKLIST

Create a checklist of details that are likely to be affected during the transition from stage version and live version, and move those tasks to the top of the list of things to retest.

BEGIN RETESTING. Immediately have the internal team retest major features and functionality. Because technology is never foolproof, small things that no one can explain can go wrong. It just happens. And those things are what retesting catches.

SUPPORT YOUR TEAM. As the project manager, your chief concern is creating optimal conditions for the team. Bring snacks, make a playlist, do anything to help your team work well. At times, you might even jump in and complete items on the checklist. Just remember this: If your team is there, so are you. Even if there's not much you can do, stick around until the work is done. At the end of it all, give the team high-fives and well-deserved pats on the back. And maybe a cocktail.

THINK ABOUT: High-profile launches

If the end product is high profile, make sure someone is monitoring social channels for issues. End users will frequently post complaints or comments and you want to catch these as soon as possible. If it's outside the scope of your work, coordinate with the client, their social team, or their social agency to make sure that the person managing and monitoring online communities knows how to respond to or escalate issues posted publicly.

Post-launch activities

Seeing an idea become reality is worth celebrating. Every project is different and technology is complicated, which means that *every* project is a challenge. When the end product launches, it's proof that your team met the challenge and conquered it!

Now celebrate.

How you celebrate is up to you and your team. Have a lunch, buy ice cream sandwiches, go to happy hour, or take a field trip. Whatever it is, it should be fun and carefree (the exact opposite of the launch day atmosphere).

This is a fun, superfluous moment in the project, but it's *also* a very important, human-centered part of the process. Acknowledging people, energy, and talent is not extra, it's necessary.

Give recognition

Your team did a lot of work. If appropriate for your workplace, share your team's contributions with the entire company, your department, or with your team members' supervisors. Send a note calling out how each team member helped shepherd the project to successful completion. Recognition is amazingly effective at making people feel like all the work and energy was worth it. (Worst case, just send the note to the internal project alias and acknowledge everyone's work among the group.)

INCLUDE EVERYONE

Sometimes only the core team ends up celebrating. That's shorting your team. A lot. Every contribution that made the end product happen—from pitch to programming to launch—was integral. Remember this when you send invites and dole out praise. Include everyone from the person who sold the project to the system administrator who helped launch it.

Publicize your work

People like to talk about what they made and the clients they worked with. If there's a non-disclosure agreement, you'll have to bypass the horn trumpeting, but if not, here are some tools to manage promotion.

CHECK WITH THE CLIENT FIRST. Ask the client before broadcasting the project. They may have a soft launch date (when you actually launched it) and a hard launch date (when they make the announcement).

LEAD BY EXAMPLE. Share the launch story via the company's social media channels. This shows your team how you phrase it and gives them a chance to share the post.

Project manager checkpoint

During the entire launch stage, the client's team members frequently have many of the same emotions and thoughts running through their minds as they did with staging: They're excited, anxious, and sometimes impatient. And the same can be said of the internal team. They have as much energy and emotional investment in the project as the clients themselves.

Channeling this energy into team-wide enthusiasm and positive energy maintains the excitement that was present at the beginning of the project. Right through launch, you want everyone to feel invested, involved, engaged, and excited.

Takeaways

Launch brings together a lot of technological details and just as many interpersonal ones. It encompasses the final moments to get all the details right and the process of handing everything over to the client. It's the time when the idea becomes a reality. And these final steps are as important as the first ones.

The end product is up and running, but you're not done yet!

11

PROJECT CLOSURE

That's a wrap

After a successful launch, there are post-project tasks that solidify the relationship with the client and the lessons learned throughout the project. With a few key activities, your team can move from delivery mode to relationship mode.

In this chapter, we'll discuss

- Internal assessment
- Client closure
- Long walks on the beach (or, taking care of yourself)

Projects have specific end dates, but relationships with clients don't. The steps you take after launch day are done not only to finish the project responsibly, but also to nurture the relationship you've built with the client. And like every other step along the way, thinking, planning, analyzing, and communicating are required.

Internal evaluation

Reviewing the project from a post-launch perspective gives you and the team the chance to assess how the project unfolded. In the midst of the work, it's hard to reflect on what's happening: There's always another thing to do and another thing to plan. After all the dust has settled (but not too long after) the team can more accurately and productively review how the project actually played out.

Hold a post-project team meeting

Every project has successes and mistakes, and both are learning opportunities. An official meeting gives everyone the structure and the platform to talk about what they experienced during the project and share what lessons they learned.

INVITE EVERYONE. The entire internal team should attend these meetings. Everyone has equal say in how the project goes and how it's assessed. Moreover, like when the team was planning and brainstorming risks, more eyes and minds means a more complete team perspective.

RECRUIT A HELPER

A neutral third party who wasn't on the project team can help facilitate particularly tricky project discussions. They bring an air of objectivity that makes the meeting go more smoothly.

DETERMINE THE BEST SETTING AND STRUCTURE. The goal is to facilitate open discussions about successes *and* mistakes. Creating a productive and collaborative environment will minimize blame, finger pointing, and negativity. A project that had only a few hiccups may not require a highly structured meeting. On the other hand, if a project was particularly challenging, you may want to have a bulleted list of some of the tough spots. Brainstorm what could have been handled differently to lead to better outcomes.

BE PREPARED. Have a lot of material to get the meeting started. Difficult moments and tough situations aren't something that most people are comfortable talking about. Having a lot of warm-up topics and questions can get the conversation off to a start without any one team member standing out. It's important to model the kind of behavior and constructive conversation you want to encourage.

Be sure to hold these meetings even for projects that went really well. It's instinct to only do these on projects that went up in flames, but it's beneficial to learn *why* and *how* a project went smoothly.

In the meeting, consider

- What was done well? What successes did the team have?

- What could have gone better? What were some of the tough moments, and how could they have been avoided?

- What can be learned from the way this project unfolded?

- How could the process have been more effective?

Tie up loose ends

A secondary purpose of the post-project meetings is to make sure everything is wrapped up nicely. As a project recedes in the rearview mirror, minor, but still important, details can easily be forgotten.

As you wrap up the project, consider whether

- All the documents reflect the final project landscape

- Everything can be archived as-is

- The client needs updated versions of any project documentation or correspondence

- There are assets that need to be returned to the client or third parties

Bring lessons back to each department

You want to get as much traction from the lessons learned in the post-project team meeting as you can. Each team member should take information back to his respective department within the company. That way, the rest of the people in the company have a chance to learn from projects that they didn't work on directly. Shared knowledge benefits everyone.

Hold project manager meetings

As the epicenter of activity, project managers are in the best position to go a step further with post-project assessments.

In their department meetings, project managers should specifically discuss how *the process* worked for the project. These meetings present opportunities for your process to evolve.

As project managers share more and more about strategic and tactical successes and challenges, your process will be customized to fit both your company and the different types of projects that your teams execute.

Report to leadership

REPORT RESPONSIBLY

Make sure departments know the final project information that relates to their work. For example, communicate budget challenges back to the sales team and hosting issues to the system administrators.

Create a comprehensive assessment of the project for account teams and upper management. These complete reports give decision makers and business development departments accurate portraits based on the realities of the project.

Include the successes, the lessons learned, and the factual details about budgets and timing. The goal is to help everyone understand how the project went from the logistical and personnel standpoints. Each perspective gives a different snapshot that can be useful in understanding company-wide trends.

Project manager checkpoint

Post-project internal teamwork requires openness and humility on everyone's part. Critically reviewing what happened has the potential to hurt feelings and cause tension. Focus on redirecting conversations to the project, not the individuals, to keep energy and emotions even.

TIP: Collect data for yourself

As a project manager, collect data about your projects for your own files. Having a list of the projects you managed and how successful they were are powerful tools for marketing yourself or offering as leverage in performance reviews.

Client evaluation

The purpose of the post-project client meeting is to officially mark the close of a specific part of the project. It might be a phase, or it might be the project in its entirety. Although relationships with clients never end (we hope), the project as defined in the strategy and user experience brief does have to come to a close.

Kick off the post-project relationship

All projects move beyond delivery mode. As hard as it may be, your team has to say, "We've done what we said we were going to do." You want there to be a distinct transition from project mentality to ongoing-relationship mentality.

What the post-project kickoff looks like depends on the client. Given the personality and needs that they've exhibited to date, decide what would be best and clearest for them. It could be a meeting; it could be a phone call.

The purpose is to make it clear to everyone that the client has received the promised deliverables. Without these discussions, projects can drag on through small updates or changes that come trickling in. The relationship can become difficult if the client thinks something they're requesting is part of maintenance, but your team thinks it's a new add-on. If there aren't official parameters, these small requests can affect personnel resources and end up costing money.

LOOSE ENDS

At times, training or product materials (see Chapter 10) aren't handed off to the client before launch due to a compressed timeline. Use the sign-off meeting to distribute any remaining materials they'll need to move forward.

Schedule post-project check-ins

Plan to review the product and check in with the client a few weeks after launch and again a few months later. If you feel like it's necessary, you can plan even more. It's up to your team and the client to determine the best way to keep the end product monitored and successful.

The goal is to see if the client has any issues or concerns now that the product is up and running. Before the discussion, have your team review the product to see that it's operating as everyone on your side expected and that it's being kept up in the manner that the team initially planned for. If the team sees any red flags, bring it up with the client.

Look at all aspects of the product: content, functionality, metrics, and anything else that's required to make the product and client successful.

When considering content, think about

- Whether the client is managing the content according to the plan. If not, are design or layout changes necessary?

- Whether the client or the end users are using the product in the way it was designed.

When considering metrics, think about

- Whether the analytics are set up correctly to give the client the necessary information. Hint: Look for anomalies that suggest that something is askew, like a drop in traffic right after launch, which may indicate that tracking codes aren't set up properly.

- Review the strategy and user experience brief and ensure that all the metrics you need to measure the product's performance are in place and working correctly.

Consider how the project may evolve:

- Is there a second phase of the project? If so, start planning.

- If a second phase isn't on the books, but one is happening, get a start date set now.

SECOND PHASES

When you're working on a second or third phase of a project, you're usually not creating as much from scratch; you're updating, refining, and verifying. If the features were already defined, this means looping back to the Production & Deployment phase, and bypassing the Research & Planning phase.

Project manager checkpoint

The transition from project mode to relationship mode should feel as little like goodbye as possible. The client will always be your client; the only thing that's ending is the project (and possibly only one phase of the project). As you go through the meeting and end-of-project conversations, be sure to reiterate that sentiment to the client *and* your internal team.

As the client begins to take ownership of the end product, questions will come up. Be prepared to handle that communication, whether it's walking them through everything again or (politely) putting your foot down because it's beyond scope. Both are realistic possibilities; the important thing is to know what your response should be and how to communicate it.

Until later

Once all the documents are in order, everything is passed off to the client, and the team has productively assessed the project, it's time to officially mark the end of the project for yourself.

Go for a walk, read a book, and take a break. Treat yourself to some TLC because before you know it, you'll be back in the trenches. And the better you take care of yourself, the better you can take care of your next project team.

Takeaways

Wrapping up a project takes care and consideration. Fight the urge to forge ahead without taking the time to do it right. Projects big and small, smooth and bumpy offer the team opportunities to learn and perfect their work. If you don't take the time to do this, you're not getting as much as you can from your work.

As the project concludes, remember to treat yourself, your team, and your client like people. Thank them and show them your appreciation. These human gestures bring the project to a collaborative end.

Well guys, that's it.

We set out to give you a framework for defining and delivering interactive projects successfully: approach them with goals, technology, and people in mind, not just tactics, deadlines, and milestones. Interactive projects are an essential part of our personal and professional lives, and managing them well is about much more than logistics. A good process guides—and requires—the critical thinking, communicating and analyzing that agencies, clients, and teams need to do along the path to success.

We hope our insights, questions, tips, tasks, and advice make your process and projects better. If you liked what we said, tell the Internet. If not, tell us. Either way, we'd like to hear from you.

Index